Dynamics of Virtual Work

Series Editors
Ursula Huws
De Havilland Campus
Hertfordshire Business School
Hatfield, UK

Rosalind Gill
Department of Sociology
City University London
London, UK

The book gives an original, critical and timely perspective on the socio-technical (co)design of games/3D software platforms. The uniqueness lies in the integration of an in-depth analysis of technological artefacts (toolkits, engines and interfaces) with user practices of 'modding' and the socio-economic context. The combined qualitative and quantitative research nicely dissects the intricate interdependence and dynamic between developer companies and mod developers, while indicating implications for firm-user learning opportunities and the dialectis of community and commerce. A must-read for anyone with a keen interest in the transformative potential of user participation that goes beyond typical celebrative thinking.
—Jo Pierson, *Vrije Universiteit Brussel (imec-SMIT)*

The ubiquity of user-created content on today's leading digital platforms is largely considered as an instance of democratization. While it is undeniably true that users have greater access to the means of cultural production, how user participation is integrated and understood in the industry workplace is less clear. This in-depth study of the work of "modders" of games and virtual worlds is highly instructive to survey the blurring of boundaries among actors, genres, user and firm practices and relationships. In her contribution to our understanding of the "participatory turn", Van der Graaf's draws on exciting empirical data to challenge the assumptions about the seemingly straightforward relationship between users and firms.
—David Nieborg, *University of Toronto*

Technological change has transformed where people work, when and how. Digitisation of information has altered labour processes out of all recognition whilst telecommunications have enabled jobs to be relocated globally. ICTs have also enabled the creation of entirely new types of 'digital' or 'virtual' labour, both paid and unpaid, shifting the borderline between 'play' and 'work' and creating new types of unpaid labour connected with the consumption and co-creation of goods and services. This affects private life as well as transforming the nature of work and people experience the impacts differently depending on their gender, their age, where they live and what work they do. Aspects of these changes have been studied separately by many different academic experts however up till now a cohesive overarching analytical framework has been lacking. Drawing on a major, high-profile COST Action (European Cooperation in Science and Technology) Dynamics of Virtual Work, this series will bring together leading international experts from a wide range of disciplines including political economy, labour sociology, economic geography, communications studies, technology, gender studies, social psychology, organisation studies, industrial relations and development studies to explore the transformation of work and labour in the Internet Age. The series will allow researchers to speak across disciplinary boundaries, national borders, theoretical and political vocabularies, and different languages to understand and make sense of contemporary transformations in work and social life more broadly. The book series will build on and extend this, offering a new, important and intellectually exciting intervention into debates about work and labour, social theory, digital culture, gender, class, globalisation and economic, social and political change.

More information about this series at
http://www.springer.com/series/14954

Shenja van der Graaf

ComMODify

User Creativity at the Intersection of Commerce and Community

Shenja van der Graaf
Senior Researcher at imec-SMIT
Vrije Universiteit Brussel
Brussels, Belgium

Dynamics of Virtual Work
ISBN 978-3-319-61499-1   ISBN 978-3-319-61500-4   (eBook)
DOI 10.1007/978-3-319-61500-4

Library of Congress Control Number: 2017947303

Cover illustration: Önder Özkan KILIÇ / Alamy Stock Photo

Printed on acid-free paper

This Palgrave Macmillan imprint is published by Springer Nature
The registered company is Springer International Publishing AG
The registered company address is: Gewerbestrasse 11, 6330 Cham, Switzerland

For my parents and Yuli, my light.

Acknowledgements

Over my journey of the years it took from my first interest in audience research and digital culture in the 1990s (hello LA!) and now culminating in this book, numerous people have directly or indirectly guided my Second Life.

A very big thank you for travelling with me, Robin Mansell. Her knowledge, faith, generosity, kind words and absolute professionalism have pushed me to go the extra mile. Without her this book might never have been written. Sonia Livingstone kindly shared her intellect and experience showing me that it is ok to walk many paths. For half of my life William Uricchio has been my rock. He introduced me to the academic world and set me free.

I am indebted to the Berkman Klein Center for Internet & Society (Harvard), Hakuhodo Foresight, Research Center for Information Law (University of St. Gallen), British Academy, Convergence Culture Consortium (MIT), Institute for Data Driven Design, Valve Inc., Linden Lab, OpenSim and many Second Life residents, especially Garrett Cobarr. Thank you for your support. Also, Oliver Day. Thanks goes especially to all at the Department of Media and Communications (LSE) for many inspiring years. Also, a big thank you to my wonderful colleagues at imec-SMIT (Vrije Universiteit Brussel), their support and wit in good and bad times helped me to stay put and keep smiling. In particular, Wim Vanobberghen, Carina Veeckman and Caroline Pauwels. I am forever grateful for COST Dynamics of Virtual Work and the opportunities it has given me, including this book and my son. Thank you, Ursula Huws and also Keith Randle.

The support, inspiration and challenges offered by colleagues and friends across several time zones have helped me tremendously in developing this research. David Nieborg, thank you for our unorthodox metal friendship, and Doris Rusch for being true. Jonas Breuer, thank you for being you, to have my back, and your critical eye in this endeavor.

Words are not enough to express my gratitude towards my wonderful parents, sister and family, and friends. Thank you for always believing in me and letting me be. With the door always open-wide my dad and mom offer a home-away-from-home-away-from-home-away-from-home… Thank you all for accepting my many periods of absence and true denial and allowing me to multitask between several lives. Lastly, I am indebted to Eran Fisher for his support and commitment to this project and our life-long Yuli project. In clear and muddy waters, you have been there, offering advice or just kept quiet. And the road goes on, and whither it is bound, I do not know.

Brussels, April 2017

Contents

List of Figures

1

Designing for Mod Development

1.1 "Hello, World!"

London, Easter Day, 2006, was the first day of my Second Life. It was the year that Second Life gate-crashed worldwide making news headlines such as Second Life Will Save Copyright (Wired, 20/11/06), Get a (Second) Life (Financial Times, 17/11/06), Talent-Spotting in Virtual World's (BBC News, 21/6/06) and A Virtual World's Real Dollars (BusinessWeek, 28/3/06).[1] The reason it gained so much attention was that Second Life, developed by Linden Lab, was presented as a three-dimensional (3D) web-based environment where users, rather than the developer firm, are central to the design and maintenance of the platform. Instead of offering a developer-imposed narrative, Second Life operates as a rather open and extensible platform for development drawing in users who have an interest in participating in practices with others, bringing their competencies as artists, programmers and businessmen into their Second Life experience. Also, the intellectual property rights of these user-made contributions were said to rest in the hands of their respective creators. These features were considered a dramatic departure from what was common in the larger (3D) games and in the digital platform industry. These strategic arrangements seemed to point to a dynamic

© The Author(s) 2018   **1**
S. van der Graaf, *ComMODify*, Dynamics of Virtual Work,
DOI 10.1007/978-3-319-61500-4_1

relationship between the roles of Linden Lab and the users in the enhancement of Second Life. This warrants an investigation into the dynamics
between the developer firm and users with particular attention to the
ways the firm develops user participation into a market and the ways in
which that market enables and facilitates particular modes of user-driven
development that are shown to shape and maintain a firm-hosted platform as product and service.

While I had already heard about Second Life by 2003 at the State of
Play conference in New York and was impressed with Linden Lab's vision,
the installation disk I received did not work and, as these things go, dis-
appeared from my radar until 2006. So, on Easter morning, still in my
PJs, I installed Second Life on my Mac and created a female avatar by the
name of Rocketgrrrl Tripp.[2] The prefab avatar raised from the digital
trenches was a rather average-looking young woman dressed in jeans and
a t-shirt, so I spent some time playing around with the appearance editor.
After a while I had created Rocketgrrrl more to my liking by changing her
into a raven-black, longhaired, big-blue-eyed woman wearing black latex-
like pants and a jacket, and knee-length black boots. Now ready to
explore Second Life I tried to figure out how to walk the newcomer's
route guided by instruction signposts in such a manner that I was actually
able to read those signs. This was difficult. Impatiently I gave up trying to
read them and checked out the interface menu instead. By clicking
around I accidentally hit 'search' and somehow arrived in a nightclub. A
very handsome punk rocker approached me and asked me whether I was
interested in making some Linden Dollars (L$) by 'camping' in the club.
I had no idea what he meant. I tried to sit down on a bar stool next to
him, but one of my legs was not bending and my arms extended above
my head as if I wanted to reach for the disco ball on the ceiling. Time to
log off. Nearly six hours had passed. Still puzzled by what it was that I
actually had been doing in Second Life I could not come up with any-
thing other than 'not much'.

That same evening, however, I logged back on and found myself still
in the same nightclub and I was relieved to notice that my posture had
returned to normal. Not knowing where to go, and knowing only that I
did not feel like staying in the club, I stumbled outside and, like a
drunken person, tried to walk without bumping too much into things

over vast lands filled with avatars, shops, residential houses, parks, boats and emptiness. What I encountered was mostly in a state of 'under construction'. Right there and then, I could see avatars on their land chatting, using lingo like 'rezzing' and suddenly new objects would appear from out of nowhere. I spent that evening just standing here and there to watch other avatars build. That experience would exemplify the way I was going to spend most of my Second Life. It is during those times that I encountered and talked to other users, in all shapes and sizes, building, texturing and scripting a living and a social life in the various corners of the platform.

From early on it was clear that the creative capacity of Second Life could be evidenced in these practices of development, customization and visual socialization that were made possible by purposively firm-designed systems; the so-called editor or toolkit, that put modification activities in the hands of users. This has resulted in a thriving 3D environment that allowed for vibrant social interactions, knowledge exchanges and the improvement and development of 3D products and services contributing new dimensions to the Second Life experience.

Today, thirteen years after its inception, Second Life's overall popularity has waned and shifted to other platforms that may operate and look much better. Yet, to this day, it can be seen as a forerunner of a firm-hosted platform that thrives on user-generated content (or, data) wielding a microcosm for Internet and real-life culture. Arguably, Second Life may still be ahead of its time possessing an entire market it created itself. Facilitating a firm-hosted platform that serves about 1 million users monthly (a mixture of regular users and first timers),[3] Second Life tells a story of content creation, connectivity and commodification between the developer firm and user communities indicative of tensions such as those about exploitation and privacy we are currently facing online associated with the transition from user-based to market-based platforms like Facebook. In this book I aim to uncover the underlying complexities by concentrating on what constitutes user participation on a firm-hosted platform.

In examining the colourful history of Second Life in its heyday, attention is drawn to revealing the dynamic between user communities and the developer firm as co-participants in platform development practices and advancements that may occur over time. My aim is to lay bare structures and norms for participation and organization of practices across firm boundaries in which particular contemporary challenges are demarcated in addition to the technological and socio-economic structures through which they are facilitated and maintained (Berdou 2011; Carpentier and Dahlgren 2014; cf. Mansell 2012). The firm-hosted 3D platform represents here a public site where norms and values—and, therefore, rules and regulations—are shaped and disputed reigning and nurturing the emerging realm of platforms (van Dijck 2013). My objective is to detect trajectories of 'community and monetization', of, for example, what is considered top-down and bottom-up, professional and amateur, cooperation and exploitation, that are emergent aspects of the so-called platformization of the Internet (Helmond 2015; Srnicek 2017). It is this migration between digital developer firms via their platform strategies and user participation via their creative endeavours or, labour practices that I aim to systematically describe in this book, as the impact for society is significant.

1.2   Approaching the Playground

The relationship between fan and producer, then, is not always a happy or a comfortable [one]. […] Yet fans have nevertheless found ways to turn the power of the media to their own advantage and to reclaim media imagery for their own purposes. (Jenkins 1992: 32)

The hardest question we'll have to answer is whether we will attempt to thwart this burgeoning online creativity […] in the name of protecting crumbling institutions, or foster it, and the participatory culture it can lead us to. (Palfrey and Gasser 2008: 129)

The early expectation that Web 2.0 technology was going to usher in a platformed sociality conditioned by user equality and equal access turned out to be utopian. […] all platforms treat some users as more equal than others owing to the hierarchical system inscribed in their interface designs. […] The potential empowerment […] thus presented itself as a double-edged sword. (van Dijck 2013: 159)

It is well known that users engage in the production of meaning, of cultural texts, and technology itself. Since the 1990s, researchers have shown an increasing interest in the linkage between new technologies and users, looking in particular at the formation of new social collectivities and 'bottom-up' redefinitions of creative practices, often vis-à-vis corporate-produced or provided content (Jenkins 1992; Klein 1999). More specifically, they have tended to yield insight into (illegal) practices where users take basic materials provided by commercial firms and actively reappropriate and redistribute those materials as creative products, accounting for the seemingly changing social and economic arrangements of the more traditional division of labour between production and consumption (Banks 2013; Bruns 2008; Hesmondhalgh 2010). An important thread in these discussions concerns the dynamics of user participation as a significant aspect of the knowledge-based economy (OECD 2005; United Nations 2008) or of broad terms such as the network society (Castells 2001), the learning economy (Lundvall and Johnson 1994), or the information society (cf. Crawford 1983; Foray 2004; Fuchs 2007; Robins and Webster 1999). All these concepts emphasize the prominent role of information and knowledge, and the use of digital information and communication technologies associated with new opportunities for user participation in digital content development.

The impetus for this book was evidence of the so-called 'participatory turn' in user participation in digital development practices (OECD 2007). The participatory turn highlights the convergence of production, distribution and consumption practices and a blending of creativity, collaboration, sharing-enabled and sharing-assisted network technologies associated with pervasive, knowledge-intensive and information-rich user-created content activities (UN 2012). Arguably, spearheaded by the open source model of software development associated with the bazaar and gift-giving models (Berdou 2011; Raymond 1999), the rapidly evolving user-generated development of intangible goods or products is reflected in the claimed democratization of web technologies. Due to affordable and accessible tools for content production and distribution, user participation has since been emerging as a creative infrastructure. This trend is continuing with the current generation of digital platforms that increasingly offer people means to participate in adding to existing and creating new digital contents, attracting their own publics (van Dijck 2013).

In many cases, participatory web sites or platforms represent successful illustrations of a rapidly evolving, yet, often subtle, relationship of collaboration with users across firm boundaries at a time where it has become 'increasingly clear that the Internet is not only embedded in people's lives but that with the rise of a more "participative web" its impacts on all aspects of economic and social organization are expanding' (OECD 2007: 15) coinciding with a strong interest and awareness of the importance of firm engagement with those active users.

In scholarly literature and beyond, the most dominant discourse concerning user participation revolves around the notion of Web 2.0 (O'Reilly 2005), which foremost describes a shift from static to dynamic Internet content delivery when putting digital tools, applications and services into the hands of users to capture 'the wisdom of crowds' (Surowiecki 2004), or 'collective intelligence' (Lévy 1997). Many terms, concepts and models have been coined to capture the 'participatory turn' associated with Web 2.0. One stream of thought mainly investigates how logics of consumption are being reworked. Here, particular attention is paid to content or data curation to capture changing dynamics along the axis of user creativity, resulting in 'convergence culture' (Jenkins 2006); 'culture of connectivity' (van Dijck 2013); 'like economy' (Gerlitz and Helmond 2013); 'collaborative consumption' (Belk 2014); 'produsage' (Bruns 2008); 'prosumption' (Ritzer and Jurgenson 2010); 'sharing economy' (Martin 2015; Sundararajan 2016); and 'wikinomics' (Tapscott and Williams 2006).

These terms approach users as active Internet contributors who put in a certain amount of creative effort, or 'labour'. User participation in creative (or, creation) practices has become a large-scale phenomenon. User creativity is often informal, occurring in contexts where there appears to be no (apparent) authoritative entity and users voluntarily perform unassigned 'work tasks' (cf. Wendel de Joode 2005; Raymond 1999), delivered by so-called 'amateurs', 'hobbyists' and 'fans' as their input tends to be produced outside the professional realm (Jeppesen 2004; Keen 2007; Postigo 2008). This 'user environment' is often either somewhat underregulated, leaving, for example, issues of copyright, commercialization prospects and personal information in the hands of, mostly, (large) organizations who own or host the platform and use this information to their own benefit (e.g., third party sales, target advertisements), or instead it is subjected to over regulation. Within this context, user participation has evoked debates in the social, economic and policy domains that may be associated with increased user autonomy and diversity, new forms of media, different ways of doing business and the need to address policy issues such as broadband access, privacy protection and intellectual property protection (Marsden 2011; Green 2008; Leadbeater and Miller 2004). In addition, some studies suggest the ubiquity of opportunities for user participation that are accessible to 'all' and that empower the users (Burgess 2007). Others see the linkage of web tools and applications to user positions as 'a brave new world where the spirits of commonality are finally merged with the interests of capitalism' (van Dijck and Nieborg 2009: 856). The idea of a participatory web seems to have become attached to a certain 'magic' or 'hype' and concrete claims and instances of such empowerment are implied rather than manifest in the empirical evidence (cf. Woolgar 2002). Little attention has been given, for example, to factors and distinctive relationships involved in different participatory modalities, to differences between more active and passive users, while technical and social designs are claimed to lead 'magically' to building a critical mass of participation (Beer 2009; Burgess 2007; Li and Bernoff 2008).

A second stream of thought that can be distinguished in the field focusses on multisided business models associated with platforms, which are characterized by changes in technologies, social (production) practices and economic organization linked to user creativity and knowledge. Commercial strategies that aim to involve two or more distinct user groups while enabling interactions between them are referred to as 'multisidedness'. Digital platforms, established to commercially harness sociality and user creativity (or labour) in one domain, develop a multiplatform strategy overtime that can contain and cater to (various) user groups. One can thus argue that these platforms are tweaked in response to their users' needs and their owners' objectives as well as in reaction to competing platforms (Feenberg 2009) rather than being finished products or services. Google and Facebook are the most prominent examples here.

Google bought YouTube (2006) and Waze (2013), and Facebook bought Whatsapp (2014) and Instagram (2012), adding to their spectrum hugely popular user-driven (video, navigation, messaging and photo) service applications, together with expertise and a fast-growing user community. How far or close an organization is from a multisided economic model carries significant economic trade-offs (Hagiu and Wright 2015). As a result, the boundaries and the main interface of platforms like Facebook, Airbnb, and Steam (Valve Inc.) are in constant flux, underpinning various competitive efforts that may not necessarily benefit or support an unbundled and open market (Ballon and Heesvelde 2011).

In short, a series of practices involving firm-hosted digital platforms can be detected, which mark a transition from a user-based to market-based orientation, thereby highlighting a migration between developer firms and user participation in labour practices. Understanding this enables us to unravel emergent aspects of the so-called platformization of the Internet, so as to get to grips with shifting or new norms and mechanisms for user participation as well as values of creativity (or, labour) associated with the trajectories of community and commerce. The way norms and mechanisms on the platform are constituted and maintained, and with what implications for product development across firm boundaries, underpin the construction of participation and creativity and are precisely what is at stake in the struggle over the emerging domain of platforms (cf. Mansell 2016).

The focus of this book is guided by the interwoven observations associated with the claimed democratization of the Internet and the continuous interoperability and decentralization of platforms and their features (cf. Helmond 2015; van Dijck et al. 2016). In addressing these aspects that have remained largely unexplored in the user-participation literature, the main theoretical framework is supported by several insights developed in work on communities of practice and user-centred innovation associated with recent platform and app studies (cf. Nieborg 2015). More specifically, with its focus on active media spectatorship, collaboration and creativity, the media research literature has made many valuable contributions relevant to the topics investigated, while insufficient attention has been given to the development and organization of firm-user relationships on firm-hosted platforms where both commercial and non-commercial production modalities interact to underpin product development. This may be due to a rather functional understanding of (networked) user participation, which cannot fully explain the growing significance of the role of user communities in knowledge production and innovation in the context of the developer firm. Also, existing user-participation literature about these firm–user interactions has tended to be based frequently on intuitive claims about user participation and there is so far only an incomplete picture of the role of user participation in these commercial environments. Moreover, analyses have tended to focus on the interactions between users and technology or on organizational socio-economic structures instead of offering a more holistic perspective (van Dijck 2013).

However, my investigation is not about the aesthetic and social qualities of user participation or the technological characteristics of software modularity, interoperability, or the wider innovation system that underpins such developments. Rather, it is about specific aspects of platform-as-product or service development across firm boundaries illuminating the growing significance of user communities in knowledge production and innovation that are associated with the emerging knowledge-based economy. Consequently, this book aims to yield insight into the dynamics between the developer firm and users with particular attention to the ways the developer firm changes user participation into a market and the ways in which that market enables and facilitates particular modes of user-driven development that are shown to shape and maintain a firm-hosted platform as a site at which the developer firm can be seen to learn from its user base.

Therefore, a supporting theme is offered by the communities of practice perspective, which assists in the investigation of learning relationships between the developer firm and users underpinning product development across firm boundaries (Lave and Wenger 1991). Participation in user communities can be approached in terms of enculturation practices such as apprenticeship and mastery. On the basis of shared beliefs and common interests communities are formed, and work towards enculturating newcomers into communal belief systems, skills and practices from those who have already mastered the group's social and material practices. In addition, such web-based communities have been found to be effective in enabling and facilitating (voluntary) knowledge sharing (Foray 2004). Through these networked communities of practice people are said to develop and share the capacity to create and employ knowledge that can assist in advancing user creativity that underlies the organization of product development (Nonaka et al. 2000). More specifically, through participation and practices, users can exchange information and are regarded as being part of the firm's dynamic knowledge base, arguably providing the firm with opportunities to learn (Wenger 1998). This information-based and practice-based perspective is therefore expected to yield insight into the underlying dimensions of the growth of knowledge and sharing practices across firm boundaries with the aim of highlighting knowledge contributions as a potential source of competitive advantage (Freeman 1991).

The literature concerning user-centred innovation provides another supporting theme (von Hippel 2005). In a more traditional view of innovation, firms take on most, if not all, product development, while, in the users-as-innovators model, users are viewed as valuable innovators in the stages of idea generation and the process of product development (Jeppesen 2004). Following the line of argument associated with rapidly expanding user participation and enhanced networked connectivity, consulting with users has become an important focal point for firms. As previously mentioned, this involving of multiple stakeholders with a focus on users is often organized in multisided platform business models, which are characterized by multisided market effects. These describe how platforms internalize positive externalities created at the sides (Armstrong 2006). In other words, each participating group profits from the usage, directly or indirectly, because others are participating, each side being able to exist because of its counterparts. Multisided markets are thus subject to network effects; the more people using them, the better they get (Evans 2010). Consequently, firms appear to be actively encouraging and facilitating user participation in the innovation process, which may be evidenced in purposively designed and provided toolkits. Providing toolkits for innovation and (co-)design is a means of systematically outsourcing certain design and innovation tasks from the firm to the user, assisting users in improving and developing new products and services (von Hippel 2005). In this way, users are presented with a broader palette to participate, better equipping them to advance and develop products according to their own interests and needs, while contributing to product development.

From this theoretical lens, the developer firm may be seen to benefit from a relatively low-cost approach to acquiring user-provided information such as user-contributed ideas, improvements and developments of products and services underpinning the overall knowledge base of the firm. With many accounts in the user-centred innovation literature having developed an individualistic approach to users-as-innovators such as in the investigation of motivations for innovating and ways of contributing, and with a somewhat narrow understanding of communities of practice involving ideas of community membership, user and firm 'cultures' have been rather simplistically addressed in these traditions compared to in the user-participation literature.

Against this backdrop, this book offers a multifaceted, multidisciplinary approach integrating these lines of research in support of addressing the main argument presented here in the examination of Second Life.

1.3 All the Games That Are Fit to Mod

Worldwide, millions of players make the overall games industry a socially significant and high risk, technologically advanced, capital intensive, proprietary practice as well as a billion dollar industry.[4] This industry develops games that can be played on consoles (e.g., Xbox One by Microsoft, Wii U by Nintendo or PlayStation 4 by Sony) and handhelds (e.g., PlayStation Vita by Sony or Nintendo 3DS by Nintendo); computer games such as Call of Duty: Black Ops by Activision; games that engage in online massively multiplayer online role-playing (MMORPGs) such as World of Warcraft by Blizzard Entertainment; and mobile application games (e.g., Candy Crush by King Digital Entertainment).[5] Contemporary devices offer a 'cross-over' of services allowing gamers to use multiple devices, compete online and download content such as game demos, TV shows and movies, as well, increasingly, allowing them to change or add content fitting the participatory web phenomenon.

User participation or creativity in the games software industry has enthusiasts and amateur developers tinkering with their favourite games despite the inherent complexity of game development. For games it is commonly referred to as *modding*, short for the practice *of modifying* a game executed by a *modder* (or, *mod developer*) with a *modification* or *mod* as outcome[6] (cf. 'hacker' in Levy 2001; Raymond 1999). Both hardware and software can be modified. There exist many variants of game software modifications varying from partial conversions like gameplay mods, such as slightly altered maps or skins, to game-additions (or 'add-ons') such as server tools or single-player missions, and to total conversion modifications.[7] Thus, user participation in mod development can be approached as a practice where 'creativity is any act, idea, or product that changes an existing domain, or that transforms an existing domain into a new one' and a creative individual is 'someone whose thoughts or actions change a domain, or establish a new domain' (Csikszentmihaly 1996: 25–26). Also, user participation in this context points to a non-zero-sum collaborative effort where 'a new whole is forming' by contributions made by mod developers that 'could not have been generated if the efforts had been individualistic' and subsequently 'the "non-zero-sumness" of collaboration therefore does not stipulate that such an outcome is greater or better, but rather different' (Elliott 2007: 33).

Contemporary game genres seem to constitute a participatory design where users are increasingly approached as important components of development, mainly a computer(PC)-centred affair. It seems that the PC-based genres First Person Shooter (FPS) and role-playing games are most frequently modified (Jeppesen 2004). In particular, FPS has 'a strong history of fan involvement in modification' (Postigo 2008: 60), so far that the FPS mod culture has arguably become 'institutionalized'. Technologically advancing the games is a common interest of developer firm and mod developers, which 'may well contribute to the ongoing technological interplay between both parties' (Nieborg 2005: 3).

Over the past decade or so, we have witnessed a rapidly growing PC-based mod format associated with 3D collaborative, world-building developments that are less game-like. Virtual worlds and especially 3D collaborative platforms have moved away from some FPS attributes towards an architecture that is more similar to the Internet (and in particular, its Web 2.0 features) but with 3D simulation features. In those virtual environments, user experiences arise from user-generated content as well as from structured experiences associated with many PC games (such as quests in a narrative form) (van der Graaf 2012a). Second Life is the earliest popular and emblematic example. Such virtual worlds (or MMORPGs) are persistent, open-ended, 3D online environments enabled by relatively cheap and fast Internet connections and advanced graphics of current devices (Castronova 2005; Steinkuehler 2005). They constitute the vanguard of a new generation of gaming; persistent, graphically advanced (re)presentation, interactivity where users' actions affect the results of other users' (through their avatars), adhering to the laws of physics, accommodating simultaneous access for a large number of players, and utilizing an exchange system of virtual assets (such as currency, items and realty). A further distinction can be made between virtual worlds and 3D collaborative platforms, as the former focusses on a game aspect in a world, while the latter are thoroughly malleable and world-building oriented. 3D platforms also tend to be more community based. If any narration is available it is likely to be created by users (cf. Yee 2006).

Against this backdrop, increasingly game/3D development seems to suggest a co-construction of game/3D development occurring between developer firm and mod developers (Banks 2013; Taylor 2006). To potentially benefit from user participation in development practices of both hardware and software, the developer firm needs to open up, providing access to software, tools and (parts of) the underlying technology, which is often supported by dispersing information via wikis and manuals. It then also needs to provide a (semi-)legal framework to facilitate and regulate user-generated contributions (Frederiksen 2006; Nieborg and van der Graaf 2008).[8]

Toolsets or toolkits are specialized software applications necessary for particular parts of the game development process, such as level editing and script compilation (Prügl and Schreier 2006; West and Gallagher 2006). There are specific *within-firm toolsets*, provided by the firm as tools developers need to work. These tools may be internally designed or third-party developed like commercial off-the-shelf graphics packages (e.g., Maya, Photoshop). *End-user toolkits* are developed and provided by the developer firm, either completely identical to within-firm tools, or specifically designed for end user. Also third party tools can be provided with the product or (if allowed and compatible) used on the modder's own initiative. And lastly, again if allowed and possible, mod developers may develop their own tools to mod the game, world, or platform. Furthermore, both first- and third-party toolkits may be located internal and external to the game/3D environment (van der Graaf 2012a).

Although tools are often custom released for a specific environment, they might be reused for other games and other 3D settings (i.e., internally developed, licensed to third-party developers and mod communities). For example, game developer Valve has included its Source Development Kit (SDK) with first-party tools such as Faceposer, Valve Hammer editor, Half-Life Model Viewer and third-party tool Softimage|XSI EXP, which was also used internally to develop the FPS Half-Life 2. In addition, for some tools (part of) the source code is also available such as for the Half-Life Model Viewer that enables users to mod the Viewer toolkit itself as well (Nieborg and van der Graaf 2008).

Toolkits may or may not be provided with the game, virtual world, or 3D collaborative platform. The release of toolkits seems to be part of an industry-wide trend, coinciding with low-cost digital distribution platforms (van der Graaf 2012a; cf. Nieborg 2011). Not only toolkits enable user participation. In particular, for FPS, the game engine—which is the proprietary technology of the firm—can fulfil that function as it tends to consists of a modular design,[9] and is typically used as development platform for other games, in-house or licensed to third-party developers (Bogost 2007). For example, Valve's source engine is the used for the Half-Life 2 series, the sequel Team Fortress 2 and Portal, while the Unreal Engine 3 was used by 2K Games to develop Bioshock and the US Army used it for America's Army 3.0 (van der Graaf 2012b). Not many developer firms, however, open up their engine for mod development nor can the engine technology itself be modded. Typically, mod developers get access to (parts of the) game code and a firm-designed toolkit that allow them to customize and design essential parts of the game.[10] The game engine is thus not 'infinitely adaptable' nor 'content neutral' (Dovey and Kennedy 2006: 57).

For virtual worlds or more 3D collaborative platforms such as World of Warcraft (Blizzard Entertainment) and Minecraft (Mojang AB) not the game engine but rather the client-server system and interface become more apparent mechanisms. Here, an often free Internet application may be run on a client-server system architecture for which the client software needs to be purchased. Users install client software on their computers in order to connect to remote server software that continuously runs the virtual world. In order to run these environments network protocols, security (e.g., to prevent cheating; cf. Consalvo 2007) and a (relational) database design must be in place.[11] The system architecture of many virtual worlds is such that the world is run on separate servers (commonly referred to as 'shards', cf. McFarlane 2005). It means that the world is split up into a number of parallel environments through clustered servers, all of which run parallel instances of the same world but with different sets of users (Ye and Cheng 2006).[12] A topologically tiled grid can also be deployed which is the case for Second Life, and which connects the 'four nearest neighbours' simulators to look after the physics, run scripts, manage the objects and the overall land within a fixed square region of space (Rosedale and Ondrejka 2003). So, when objects move around the physically simulated platform, their representation is transferred (along with, for example, scripts, objects, and textures) from simulator to simulator when they cross over the 'boundaries'.

In these systems mod development tends to be enabled and facilitated by the developer firm's Application Programming Interfaces-based user customization tools. These tools usually can only be used to mod the user interface via so-called 'add-ons' (i.e., files located in the mod developer's game folder that enhance her/his interaction with the virtual world) and 'macros' (i.e., combinations of actions that are executed in one go).[13] Third-party tools, 'outside-world' developed macros and the like may be allowed too. If not, these are considered 'exploits' and can lead to some kind of punishment, and even to being banned (Consalvo 2007). Users can thus have full control over the 'look and feel' of toolbars, hot keys, macros and so forth that assist in making alterations to, for example, the built-in player, menu buttons, or even the standard interface to induce its functionality. Furthermore, mods can be stand-alone, built on libraries, and can be a combination of several individually created mods.

The role of engines, toolkits and interfaces thus show that there exist several formats of game designs characterized by a perpetual state of development and allow users to be creative or innovative in different participatory modes and ways (Haddon 2005; Sotamaa 2005). Achieving mod developers to participate in creative practices is directly connected to the user's own, shared participation in mod development within the boundaries set by the developer firm. Put aptly by Benkler (2006: 75) 'the commercial provider offered a platform and tools, while the users wrote the story lines, rendered the "set," and performed the entire play.' User-generated content as mod development is therefore the heart of the experience and malleable within the boundaries set by the developer firm.

1.4   'You Only Live Twice'[14]

This book uses Second Life as its main case study to investigate user participation in a segment of the 3D software industry.[15] As explained earlier, Second Life is considered to be a forerunner of a firm-hosted platform that thrives on user participation and creativity. According to the Terms of Service (ToS) Linden Lab perceives its own role as that of service provider in enabling and facilitating online user interactions on a platform where users, gratis or for a subscription fee, are free to choose, develop and modify the service environment.[16] This seems to push Second Life in the direction of approaching an advanced level of a social network service that is intertwined with 3D attributes.

More specifically, Second Life is a web-based 3D collaborative platform that constitutes the so-called Second Life Viewer, or, client application. The Viewer enables its user (also known as 'residents') to access and interact with the platform and others.[17] The Viewer is similar to a web browser à la Firefox in that both are software applications that connect to web servers ('the grid') and retrieve, or render, respectively, content or web pages on the user's screen. Thus, the Viewer looks after the display and interaction of users with text, (moving) images, sound and so forth located in Second Life or a web page. Second Life has also a built-in toolkit, that is, the 'browser' and 'tool' functionalities are integrated allowing users to build, script and texture. Certain graphics, animations and sounds can also be externally created such as with third-party animation editors, and uploaded into Second Life. The underlying technologies used are a mixture of proprietary, free and open-source software.

Second Life has been marked as a particularly radical model of user participation in digital development practices, where any Jane Doe or a powerful firm can engage in mod development highlighting an environment that is home to different levels of power, wealth and influence underlying software development, entrepreneurship, education, philanthropy, and politics. Second Life is a firm-hosted collaborative platform where firm-users can 'acquire, share, and build knowledge [that] dramatically impact the rate of innovation for all who use them. [It] can change innovation everywhere. By creating a culture of experimentation, exploration, and collaboration, [Second Life] makes radically decentralized approached, reduced costs, and collaboration across geographic distance available to those with access' (Ondrejka 2007: 27–28).

In practice, Second Life has allowed users to access vast stretches of land and islands that can be used for seemingly endless possibilities such as building a shop front, renting out a music venue to performing artists, a gathering space where avatars can take classes, form self-help groups to discuss depression or still-birth, or establishing a disaster simulation environment to train rescue workers for real threats like terrorist attacks. In this capacity, Second Life offers numerous ways for people to 'immerse in products' which, especially in 2006, attracted many companies and non-profit organizations as it made Second Life an ideal platform for direct interaction, feedback' and promotion.

Reuters, for example, was quick to set up its digital headquarters, Adidas opened a retail space, BBC Radio 1 has held live broadcasts such as Radio 1's Big Weekend, IBM has used the platform as a meeting space (both internally at IBM and externally with clients), Philips has used its digital office for consumer feedback and testing, the Berkman Center for Internet & Society has live-streamed events such as luncheons and lectures in-world, and Sony BMG owned a building to promote and sell music downloads. Real money can be made through Second Life's currency, the Linden Dollar (L$) which is connected to the Exchange Market (LindeX) where users can convert earned L$ to real US Dollars (and vice versa).

Second Life thus illustrates how inputs for development arise outside the boundaries of Linden Lab. In other words, Linden Lab has offered a collaborative, multisided platform where individual users and Linden employees ('Lindens') intersect, constituted around communication of shared practices and platform (or product) use and, in this capacity, create opportunities for individual and collective development to take place. As the key technological features seem easily transferable and the mode of communication is relatively low cost, the conditions are likely to favour the formation and function of an active community of contributors. In such a set-up Linden Lab and Second Life users may share knowledge, ideas and innovations, organizing and facilitating dispersed users to collaborate, share information and learn about product use. From Linden Lab's perspective, Second Life seems to allow for a low-cost interface to its users through which they can monitor what particular users do, how they communicate about problems and needs, how alterations are made by users, and what appear to be the most urgent issues among Second Life users. Particularly, development-related information, provided and exchanged on the platform and on Second Life web sites (such as the blog and forums), and the contributions themselves can guide the observation of ways in which Linden Lab invites and supports user participation in content, front end (interface) and back end (other source code) mod development practices.

By drawing on a mixture of quantitative and qualitative data and methods, this book reveals the pivotal role of users and employed developers in the design, development and sustainability of platform design processes.[18] Three analytical categories have been developed to expose emerging relationships between the distinctive creative capacities of users and the range of capabilities afforded by the firm-provided platform that underpin the advancement of Second Life. These categories are 'design capabilities', 'design space' and 'learning by design' and refer to actions that give form to specific types of systemic participation associated with certain norms and values, which, I argue, underlie the organization and firm-user dynamics in the work involved in 3D platform design across firm boundaries. The following chapters aim to systematically demonstrate how the organization and accomplishment of work as well as the patterns of participation of modders and employed developers across firm and platform boundaries are emerging as distinct socio-economic spaces with unique production capabilities, at a time where the implications for society and culture in general are significant.

1.5 Playlist: Organization of the Book

The 'playlist' supporting the remainder of this book is organized into six chapters.

Chapter 2: 'Participation and Platformization at Play' introduces user participation literature, thereby focusing on the intertwining of relatively cheap and easy-to-use web technologies, facilitating user creativity and participation in digital development practices and a growing number of firms that seek to lever and promote user participation on their web-based platforms. First, it discusses and assesses topics concerning participation in cultural production, commerce and labour that seem to underpin a reworking of the organization of firm-user relationships. Second, it examines research that links user creativity to a knowledge-based view of the firm. User participation is shown to signal practices of peer production that offer opportunities for collective learning in what has been termed communities (or, networks) of practice. Lastly, the chapter focuses on the subsidiary understanding of user participation as actively engineering a distinctive aspect of the domain of innovation that situates innovation across permeable boundaries of the firm. Particular attention is drawn to toolkits for user innovation. This is situated in discussions concerning who, why and what users innovate; modularity and generativity; and entrepreneurship. In conclusion, the chapter contextualizes these lines of research by developing a conceptual framework elaborating a platform perspective.

Chapter 3: 'Game Changer' presents empirical findings concerning the design capabilities of Second Life users. First, it introduces the design capabilities as a unit of analysis. This is followed by drawing out the development of Second Life from inception to the contemporary platform of creativity, community and collaboration. Insight is yielded into the underlying drivers for users to join Second Life and six membership clusters based on several participation characteristics are developed. The chapter also offers an examination of Linden Lab and mod developers in the context of entrepreneurship. Different modes of user participation are related to organizational characteristics and culture of the developer firm. The chapter ends with highlighting key findings and yields some terms such as participation tipping point.

Chapter 4: 'Of Toolkits, Engines and Interfaces' presents empirical findings with respect to the design space. The design space is the area for user participation in mod development practices. The analysis examines characteristics of the Second Life platform yielding insight into the functionalities of the design space associated with the firm-provided toolkit that enables and facilitates user participation. It does so by combining qualitative and quantitative data linking the workings of Second Life to three areas of user participation in mod development. More specifically, the micro-level design space focuses on in-world creative contributions, the meso-level design space addresses interface modding of the open sourced Second Life Viewer software, and the macro-level design space yields insight into mod developer groups interested in open sourcing the platform's underlying technology. This is followed by connecting the three areas of development to ways mods can be transferred, integrated and used on the Second Life platform. The conclusion draws together the main points of analysis, connects them to the findings of the design capabilities and discusses their wider implications.

Chapter 5: 'Learning and the Imperative of Production in Mod Development' presents the empirical analysis of knowledge contributions made by users and employees of Linden Lab. The analysis yields insight into user participation on the firm-hosted platform by linking the design capabilities and design space to various communication practices. First, the relational dimension of mod development associated with firm-user learning is introduced. This is followed by an analysis of learning practices among the developer firm and mod developers on the firm-hosted platform. In particular, mastery and leadership practices are highlighted. Furthermore, learning is connected to the aspect of 'production' underlying user participation, because throughout this research, it has been suggested that 'production' continues well after the release of the platform by user contributions made to the design space, emphasizing several interactions among contributors across firm boundaries. More specifically, the findings demonstrate that Second Life is a site where various contributions by both users and the developer firm generate ideas about discovering, developing and refining creative practices associated with firm learning that contribute to ongoing product development. The concluding remarks draw attention to the centripetal effect of complex learning among mod developers and the firm.

Chapter 6: 'Second Life between Participation and Competition' provides an analytical synthesis of the results concerning production modalities underlying firm-user interactions on the firm-hosted platform and considers this in the light of the framework developed for this book and broader theoretical implications. It argues that the lines of analytical investigation involving user participation in mod development practices presented in Chapters 3, 4 and 5 contribute to an understanding of a redefinition of a particular configuration of overlapping production modalities of the developer firm and users. Several terms, such as modification effect market, are developed to identify this type of firm-user relationship in the context of the 3D software industry.

Chapter 7: 'Commodify! And Beyond' concludes this book with a contemplation of the main research findings in the wider context of participation and platforms, thereby highlighting issues such as public value as an opportunity for further research.

Notes

1. See http://secondlife.com/news/ for Second Life news archives and press releases between 2002 and 2017.
2. An *avatar* is usually a prefab or self-created digital persona controlled by the user. It enables users to participate and interact in games and other game-like environments.
3. See http://motherboard.vice.com/read/why-is-second-life-still-a-thing-gaming-virtual-reality (accessed 01/12/2016).
4. See Entertainment Software Association's Essential Facts Report (2016): http://essentialfacts.theesa.com/Essential-Facts-2016.pdf (accessed 01/12/2016).
5. See for an introduction into games, culture and industry, for example, Kerr (2006), Williams and Smith (2007), Huntemann and Aslinger (2013), Ruggill et al. (2016).
6. The term *mod* has been used as umbrella for the many variants of user-generated game materials and practices neglecting to address the different functionalities among mods such as client-side maps and server-side

game stats plug-ins for First Person Shooter games. As this present study focuses on mainly one particular case study, the development of a more nuanced perspective is beyond the scope of this book.

7. Early examples are Doom (1993) and Half-Life (1999). Although there are earlier instances, game modification practices really took off in the mid- to late-1990s (Dovey and Kennedy 2006).

8. Emerging mod culture and democratization of innovation appear to go hand-in-hand, thereby highlighting that mod development is not used in a technologically deterministic way. Rather it is investigated in reciprocal firm-user dynamics evolving in practice-based communities that appear to encapsulate users-as-developers in different stages of the product life cycle.

9. Within this context, modularity also means that parts of the engine can be upgraded without 'breaking the code'.

10. Partly facilitated by the engine's modularity the developer firm tends to close off some parts of the engine for mod developers, this in contrast to third party licensees and first party developers.

11. See http://www.gamasutra.com/features/resource-guide/ (accessed 01/12/16).

12. See http://www.technologyreview.com/Infotech/19378/?a=f (accessed 01/12/16).

13. See http://www.wowwiki.com/Interface_Customization (accessed 01/12/16).

14. You Only Live Twice (Danjaq 1967).

15. This book combines elements of the intrinsic and instrumental case study by drawing attention to the case for its own interest value and to point to some (theoretical) aspects larger than the case itself (Yin 2003).

16. See http://secondlife.com/corporate/tos.php (accessed 01/12/16).

17. See https://wiki.secondlife.com/wiki/User_Interface_Improvements (accessed 01/12/16).

18. An online survey was conducted among Second Life users, resulting in 434 responses. The survey asked respondents about general Second Life characteristics such as length and type of membership and about particular features and uses of the platform such as motivations, design, and information and communication behaviour. 'First life' demographics of users such as gender, income, and employment status were also collected. Semi-structured interviews were conducted with eight Linden Lab employees and thirteen Second Life users. The interviews with Linden

Lab employees highlighted aspects of their roles within Linden Lab, their interactions with users, and their perceptions of learning opportunities. The interviews with Second Life users addressed their interests, usage patterns, contributions to the platform, and their interactions with other users and Linden Lab employees. In addition, online documents were collected and examined thematically drawing from the Second Life blog, forums, mailing lists, and public bug tracker. The documents were used to examine the ways in which the developer firm and users interact in ways which are shown to further product development.

References

Armstrong, M. (2006). Competition in Two-Sided Markets. *The RAND Journal of Economics, 37*(3), 668–691. doi:10.1111/j.1756-2171.2006.tb00037.x.

Ballon, P., & Van Heesvelde, E. (2011). ICT Platforms and Regulatory Concerns in Europe. *Telecommunications Policy, 35*, 702–714.

Banks, J. (2013). *Co-creating Videogames*. London: Bloomsbury Academic.

Beer, D. (2009). Power Through the Algorithm? Participatory Web Cultures and the Technological Unconscious. *New Media & Society, 11*(6), 985–1002.

Belk, R. (2014). You Are What You Can Access: Sharing and Collaborative Consumption Online. *Journal of Business Research, 67*, 1595–1600.

Benkler, Y. (2006). *The Wealth of Networks: How Social Production Transforms Markets and Freedom*. New Haven: Yale University Press.

Berdou, E. (2011). *Organization in Open Source Communities: At the Crossroads of the Gift and Market Economies*. New York: Routledge.

Bogost, I. (2007). *Persuasive Games: The Expressive Power of Videogames*. Cambridge, MA: MIT Press.

Bruns, A. (2008). *Blogs, Wikipedia, Second Life, and Beyond: From Production to Produsage*. New York: Peter Lang.

Burgess, J. (2007). *Vernacular Creativity and New Media*. Unpublished Ph.D., Queensland University of Technology, Queensland.

Carpentier, N., & Dahlgren, P. (2014). Histories of Media(ted) Participation: An Introduction. *Communication Management Quarterly, 30*(Spring), 7–14.

Castells, M. (2001). *The Internet Galaxy: Reflections on the Internet, Business and Society*. Oxford: Oxford University Press.

Castronova, E. (2005). *Synthetic Worlds: The Business and Culture of Online Games*. Chicago: The University of Chicago Press.

Consalvo, M. (2007). *Cheating: Gaining Advantage in Videogames*. Cambridge, MA: MIT Press.

Crawford, S. (1983). The Origin and Development of a Concept: The Information Society. *Bulletin of the Medical Library Association, 71*(4), 380–385.

Csikszentmihaly, M. (1996). *Creativity: Flow and the Psychology of Discovery and Invention*. New York: HarperCollins.

Dovey, J., & Kennedy, H. W. (2006). *Game Cultures: Computer Games as New Media*. Maidenhead: Open University Press.

Elliott, M. A. (2007). *Stigmergic Collaboration: A Theoretical Framework for Mass Collaboration*. Unpublished Ph.D., The University of Melbourne, Melbourne.

Evans, D. (2010). *Essays on the Economics of Two-Sided Markets: Economics, Antitrust and Strategy*. http://papers.ssrn.com/sol3/papers.cfm?abstract_id=1714254

Feenberg, A. (2009). Critical Theory of Communication Technology: Introduction to Special Section. *Information Society Journal, 25*(2), 77–83.

Foray, D. (2004). *The Economics of Knowledge*. Cambridge, MA: MIT Press.

Frederiksen, L. (2006). *User Communication Driving Firm Innovation: A Communication Patterns Perspective on Personal Attributes and Communication Types in an Online User Community*. Retrieved July 16, 2007, from http://www2.druid.dk/conferences/viewpaper.php?id=540&cf=8

Freeman, C. (1991). Networks of Innovators: A Synthesis of Research Issues. *Research Policy, 20*, 499–514.

Fuchs, C. (2007). Transnational Space and the 'Network Society'. *21st Century Society, 2*(1), 49–78.

Gerlitz, C., & Helmond, A. (2013, February 4). The Like Economy: Social Buttons and the Data-Intensive Web. *New Media & Society*. Online First. doi:10.1177/1461444812472322.

Green, J. (2008). *YouTube: Online Video and Co-created Value*. Cambridge, MA: Convergence Culture Consortium, Comparative Media Studies at MIT.

Haddon, L. (2005). The Innovatory Use of ICTs. In L. Haddon, E. Mante, B. Sapio, K.-H. Kommonen, L. Fortunati, & A. Kant (Eds.), *Everyday Innovators: Researching the Role of Users in Shaping ICTs* (pp. 54–66). Dordrecht: Springer.

Hagiu, A., & Wright, J. (2015). Multi-Sided Platforms. *International Journal of Industrial Organization, 43*(11), 162–174.

Helmond, A. (2015, July–December). The Platformization of the Web: Making Web Data Platform Ready. *Social Media + Society*, 1–11. doi:10.1177/2056305115603080.

Hesmondhalgh, D. (2010). User-Generated Content, Free Labour and the Cultural Industries. *Ephemera, 10*(3/4), 267–284.

Huntemann, N., & Aslinger, B. (2013). In Critical Media Studies (Ed.), *Gaming Globally: Production, Play, and Place*. New York: Palgrave Macmillan.

Jenkins, H. (1992). *Textual Poachers: Television Fans & Participatory Culture*. London: Routledge.

Jenkins, H. (2006). *Convergence Culture: Where Old and New Media Collide*. New York: New York University Press.

Jeppesen, L. B. (2004). *Organizing Consumer Innovation: A Product Development Strategy That Is Based on Online Communities and Allows Some Firms to Benefit from a Distributed Process of Innovation by Consumers*. Unpublished Ph.D., Copenhagen Business School, Copenhagen.

Keen, A. (2007). *The Cult of the Amateur: How Today's Internet Is Killing Our Culture*. New York: Doubleday.

Kerr, A. (2006). *The Business and Culture of Digital Games: Gamework/Gameplay*. London: Sage.

Klein, N. (1999). *No Logo: Taking Aim at the Brand Bullies*. New York: Picador.

Lave, J., & Wenger, E. (1991). *Situated Learning: Legitimate Peripheral Participation*. Cambridge: Cambridge University Press.

Leadbeater, C., & Miller, P. (2004). *The Pro-Am Revolution: How Enthusiasts Are Changing Our Economy and Society*. London: Demos.

Lévy, P. (1997). *Collective Intelligence: Mankind's Emerging World in Cyberspace*. Cambridge, MA: Perseus Books.

Levy, S. (2001). *Hackers: Heroes of the Computer Revolution*. New York: Penguin.

Li, C., & Bernoff, J. (2008). *Groundswell: Winning in a World Transformed by Social Technologies*. Boston: Harvard Business Press.

Lundvall, B.-A., & Johnson, B. (1994). The Learning Economy. *Journal of Industry Studies, 1*(2), 23–42.

Mansell, R. (2012). *Imagining the Internet: Communication, Innovation, and Governance*. Oxford: Oxford University Press.

Mansell, R. (2016). *Unpacking Black Boxes: Understanding Digital Platform Innovation. Draft Information, Communication and Society*. https://www. academia.edu/30175620/Unpacking_Black_Boxes_Understanding_ Digital_Platform_Innovation

Marsden, C. (2011). *Internet Co-regulation: European Law, Regulatory Governance and Legitimacy in Cyberspace*. Cambridge: Cambridge University Press.

Martin, C. J. (2015). The Sharing Economy: A Pathway to Sustainability or a Nightmarish Form of Neoliberal Capitalism? *Ecological Economics, 121*, 149–159.

McFarlane, R. (2005). *Network Software Architectures for Real-Time Massively Multiplayer Online Games*. Unpublished Master thesis, McGill University, Montreal.

Nieborg, D. B. (2005). *Am I Mod or Not? – An Analysis of First Person Shooter Modification Culture*. Paper presented at the Creative Gamers Seminar – Exploring Participatory Culture in Gaming, University of Tampere.

Nieborg, D. B. (2011). *Triple-A: The Political Economy of the Blockbuster Video Game*. Ph.D. thesis, Amsterdam School for Cultural Analysis.

Nieborg, D. B. (2015, July–December). Crushing Candy: The Free-to-Play Game in Its Connective Commodity Form. *Social Media + Society*, 1–12.

Nieborg, D. B., & van der Graaf, S. (2008). The Mod Industries? The Industrial Logic of Non-market Game Production. *European Journal of Cultural Studies, 11*(2), 177–195.

Nonaka, I., Toyama, R., & Nagata, A. (2000). A Firm as a Knowledge-Creating Entity: A New Perspective on the Theory of the Firm. *Industrial and Corporate Change, 9*(1), 1–20.

O'Reilly, T. (2005). *What is Web 2.0*. Retrieved October 4, 2008, from http://www.oreillynet.com/pub/a/oreilly/tim/news/2005/09/30/what-is-web-20.html

OECD. (2005). *Digital Broadband Content: The Online Computer and Video Game Industry*. Paris: OECD Publishing.

OECD. (2007). *Participative Web and User-Generated Content: Web 2.0, Wikis and Social Networking*. Paris: OECD Publishing.

Ondrejka, C. (2007). Collapsing Geography: Second Life, Innovation, and the Future of National Power. *Innovations, 2*(3), 27–54.

Palfrey, J., & Gasser, U. (2008). *Born Digital: Understanding the First Generation of Digital Natives*. New York: Basic Books.

Postigo, H. (2008). Video Game Appropriation Through Modifications: Attitudes Concerning Intellectual Property Among Fans and Modders. *Convergence: The International Journal of Research into New Media Technologies, 14*(1), 59–74.

Prügl, R., & Schreier, M. (2006). Learning from Leading-Edge Customers at The Sims: Opening up the Innovation Process Using Toolkits. *R&D Management, 36*(3), 237–250.

Raymond, E. (1999). *The Cathedral & The Bazaar: Musings on Linux and Open Source by an Accidental Revolutionary* (2001 Rev. ed.). Sebastopol: O'Reilly Media.

Ritzer, G., & Jurgenson, N. (2010). Production, Consumption, Prosumption: The Nature of Capitalism in the Age of the Digital 'Consumer'. *Journal of Consumer Culture, 10*(1), 13–36.

Robins, K., & Webster, F. (1999). *Times of the Technoculture: From the Information Society to the Virtual Life*. London: Routledge.

Rosedale, P., & Ondrejka, C. (2003). *Enabling Player-Created Online Worlds with Grid Computing and Streaming*. Retrieved February 6, 2008, from www.cs.ubc.ca/~krasic/cpsc538a/papers/rosedale.pdf

Ruggill, J., McAllister, K., Nichols, R., & Kaufman, R. (2016). *Inside the Video Game Industry: Game Developers Talk About the Business of Play*. London: Routledge.

Sotamaa, O. (2005). *Have Fun Working with Our Product!: Critical Perspectives on Computer Game Mod Competitions*. Paper presented at the Proceedings of DiGRA 2005 Conference: Changing Views: Worlds in Play, Vancouver.

Srnicek, N. (2017). *Platform Capitalism*. Cambridge: Polity Press.

Steinkuehler, C. A. (2005). *Cognition & Learning in Massively Multiplayer Online Games: A Critical Approach*. Unpublished Ph.D., University of Wisconsin, Madison.

Sundararajan, A. (2016). *The Sharing Economy: The End of Employment and the Rise of Crowd-Based Capitalism*. Cambridge, MA: MIT Press.

Surowiecki, J. (2004). *The Wisdom of Crowds: Why the Many Are Smarter than the Few and How Collective Wisdom Shapes Business, Economies, Societies and Nations*. New York: Doubleday.

Tapscott, D., & Williams, A. D. (2006). *Wikinomics: How Mass Collaboration Changes Everything*. New York: Penguin.

Taylor, T. L. (2006). *Beyond Management: Considering Participatory Design and Governance in Player Culture*. Retrieved February 16, 2008, from http://www.firstmonday.org/Issues/special11_9/taylor/

United Nations. (2008). *The Global Information Society: A Statistical View*. Santiago: United Nations.

United Nations. (2012). *E-Government Survey 2012: E-Government for the People*. New York: United Nations.

van der Graaf, S. (2012a). Modonomics: Participation and Competition in Contention. *Journal of Gaming and Virtual Worlds, 4*(2), 119–135.

van der Graaf, S. (2012b). Get Organized at Work! A Look Inside the Game Design Process of Valve and Linden Lab. *Bulletin of Science, Technology & Society, 32*(6), 477–485.

van Dijck, J. (2013). *The Culture of Connectivity. A Critical History of Social Media*. New York: Oxford University Press.

van Dijck, J., & Nieborg, D. B. (2009). Wikinomics and Its Discontents: A Critical Analysis of Web 2.0 Business Manifestoes. *New Media & Society, 11*(5), 855–874.

van Dijck, J., Poell, T., & De Waal, M. (2016). *De Platformsamenleving: Strijd om Publieke Waarden in een Online Wereld*. Amsterdam: Amsterdam University Press.

van Wendel de Joode, R. (2005). *Understanding Open Source Communities: An Organizational Perspective.* Unpublished Ph.D., Technische Universiteit Delft, Delft.

von Hippel, E. (2005). *Democratizing Innovation.* Cambridge, MA: MIT Press.

Wenger, E. (1998). *Communities of Practice: Learning, Meaning, and Identity.* Cambridge: Cambridge University Press.

West, J., & Gallagher, S. (2006). Patterns of Open Innovation in Open Source Software. In H. W. Chesbrough, W. Vanhaverbeke, & J. West (Eds.), *Open Innovation: Researching a New Paradigm* (pp. 82–106). Oxford: Oxford University Press.

Williams, J. P., & Heide Smith, J. (Eds.). (2007). *The Player's Realm: Studies on the Culture of Video Games and Gaming.* Jefferson: McFarland Press.

Woolgar, S. (2002). *Virtual Society? Technology, Cyberbole, Reality.* Oxford: Oxford University Press.

Ye, M., & Cheng, L. (2006). System-Performance Modelling for Massively Multiplayer Online Role-Playing Games. *IBM Systems Journal, 45*(1), 45–58.

Yee, N. (2006). MMORPG Demographics, Motivations and Experiences of Users of Massively-Multiuser Online Graphical Environments. *Presence Teleoperators and Virtual Environments, 15,* 309–329.

Yin, R. K. (2003). *Case Study Research: Design and Methods* (3rd ed.). London: Sage.

2

Participation and Platformization at Play

2.1 Participation, Innovation, Learning

As outlined in the introduction, this book connects several lines of research focusing on participation, innovation and learning for which the theoretical and conceptual foundations are discussed and defined in this chapter. In particular, attention is drawn to user participation on digital platforms vis-à-vis labour, communities of practice and toolkits for user innovation. In conclusion, a platform perspective is developed underpinning a reworking of the organization of firm-user relationships.

Participation has become an important term in developing a framework to understand the online-user creativity practices that have emerged and have been associated with a shift in connection between online consumption and production. Since the early 1990s user creativity has been understood as a kind of cultural production, encapsulated by the term 'participatory culture', in the context of media spectatorship. Henry Jenkins (1992) coined the term to explain incremental user activity in Star Trek fandom at a time when fans tended to be considered as only marginal to the way mass media was produced and consumed. Based on ethnographic accounts Jenkins suggested that fans appropriated content from mass media, reshaping it to serve their own

© The Author(s) 2018
S. van der Graaf, *ComMODify*, Dynamics of Virtual Work,
DOI 10.1007/978-3-319-61500-4_2

needs and interests involving a continuous process of the production and manipulation of meanings.[1]

By the early twenty-first century, attention had been directed towards the increasing linkage between user participation and information and communication technologies (ICT), thereby highlighting the shifting means of wealth production in the digital economy (Allen et al. 2014; Karaganis 2007).[2] A major transition herein has been associated with Web 2.0 (O'Reilly 2005), highlighting a shift from providing sites for networked communication to offering networked sociality mostly in the form of platforms. Rich (media) content is created and shared across complex platforms hosted by digital firms that cannot exist without it. Conceptualized as 'participatory turn' (OECD 2007) it is said to underpin an apparent connection between user creativity and some kind of novel configuration between industries and consumers, essentially shifting power relations marked by questions of value (Bruns 2008; Striphas 2015; van Dijck 2013). Thus, in addition to the production of meanings, users can be seen to actively engage in shaping, altering and distributing content (Burgess 2007; Livingstone 2003). Such 'user-led online environments' seem to underpin an information-based model rather than a trichotomous industrial model of production, distribution and consumption (Bruns 2008; Jenkins 2006; Leadbeater and Miller 2004; Ritzer and Jurgenson 2010; van Dijck 2013).

The formation of new social and 'bottom-up' redefinitions of creative practices vis-à-vis commercially generated content or platforms has been under scrutiny, at a moment where we witness an increasing interest of firms—if still imperfectly understood—in user activities for reasons such as revenue opportunities and re-enforcing consumer commitments (Burgess et al. 2009). This 'collision' of firm and user interests draws attention to the interplay between the structured commercial agenda of firms and the generally differently purposed agenda and appropriations of users within participatory communities. At stake is the interplay between structure and agency that alters the logic by which both firms and users process information and content accounting for the, arguably, changing social and economic arrangements between the more traditional division of labour and between production and consumption.

Within this context, a call for a rethink of 'industry' can be heard. This is informed by the idea that participation is a multifaceted dynamic encapsulating all 'agents involved in the system, not just inherited corporate structures' as participants (Hartley 2008: 8). Closely linked to this idea is the interest in multisidedness as an emerging market economy. In economics and management literature, 'multisided markets' are where a platform enables interactions between distinct parties (Rochet and Tirole 2003). This is central to the Web 2.0 Internet economy and its participatory turn. Platforms and their providers thus mediate and coordinate between different stakeholders, which are the two (or multi) sides of the market. The utility that any user A derives from the use of the platform market is correlated to the number of users B and the converse; these network effects increase the value for all parties as more people use it (Hagiu 2014). These externalities between stakeholders are internalised by the platform (Armstrong 2006). Users, advertisers, and third-party developers are, for example, brought together by Facebook, benefiting from network effects. To facilitate and harvest the participation and creativity of their users, multisided markets need to determine the right balance between control and openness. The app store, for example, has become sustainable and valuable because it has been open to any developer complying with a set of basic rules (Ballon et al. 2010). The 'gatekeeper' role of a platform is thus a powerful one, as it controls bottlenecks in the value network, selecting and processing ideas and information (Ballon 2009).

The emphasis is on the character of the markets that organize the industry that are complex and social rather than on the character of mere inputs or outputs and competition in production or consumption (Potts et al. 2008). Such an approach joins the market and digital sociality and connectivity associated with participatory cultures together and makes an analysis possible that bridges user-technology interaction with the organizational socio-economic structure (cf. Mansell 2012). In this capacity, opportunities for innovation and learning across firm boundaries that potentially benefit (the growth of) the firm are likely to occur. Accepting this, creativity, as a mode of innovation and an area of economic activity, is not understood on an individual basis but rather is a process that is evoked in a context and organization of stakeholders, knowledge, networks and technologies (Pratt 2004; van Dijck 2013). More specifically, user participation in production (and consumption) practices is said to be constituted in networks of practitioners stressing 'information feedback' over individual preferences or price signals, suggesting a move beyond the investigation of power towards the growth of knowledge. This particular perspective draws attention to (emerging) markets that are seemingly demand-driven. Rather than a linear or causal 'chain' of production associated with a supply-driven approach, this so-called 'connective market' is viewed as a dynamic underpinned by a (relatively) open system where everybody, firms and individuals, can come up with ideas and these may be taken up and dispersed into the network and retained by commerce (cf. 'social network market' in Potts et al. (2008) and 'commons-based peer production' in Benkler (2006).

Amidst questions about how to conceptualize the relationship between user participation and the firm, one issue, in particular, concerning (free) labour demands our attention. This is discussed next.

2.2   All Work and No Play?

With the 'collision' of user participation and the commercial world, attention is increasingly directed towards the apparent link between the work put in by users and (the circumstances of) employment. More specifically, as a growing number of users, in general, and software developers, in particular, voluntarily dedicate hour after hour working for free on mod projects, research has sought to address the grey areas of work, leisure, and, to a lesser extent, ownership. More specifically, the growing number of people that (occasionally) work from home gave rise to a scholarly interest in new ways of organizing work that is more decentralized and associated with ICT (Berdou 2011; Huws 2014; Malone 2004). At the same time, the realm of creativity is upheld to be augmented suggesting a kind of talent-led economy where, 'work comes to mean much more than just earning a living [...and] appears to supplant, indeed hijack, the realm of the social, re-adjusting the division between work and leisure, creating new modes of self-disciplining producing new forms of identity' (McRobbie 2002: 99; Bilton 2007).

With creativity as a key element of cultural production, work and play appear to become increasingly blurred indicating that the organization of work cannot be understood separately from the domestic sphere concerning personal (and social) interests. For example, Lee (2007) has shown that 'creative workers' in London increasingly have a 'portfolio career' stressing a work–leisure flexibility underlying a perpetual entrepreneurial outlook to work where they 'commodify' themselves. Deuze et al. (2007: 350) have studied the working lives of 'gameworkers' and found that many make substantial sacrifices (particularly concerning working hours and copyright issues) to 'call themselves game developers'. Perhaps unsurprisingly, game developers are often hired from the mod community (Nieborg and van der Graaf 2008). By tapping into the heart of the gaming community developer firms appear to aim to incorporate those gamers/developers with the passion, skills and drive to make only the best of the best. As diverse and industry-wide successful hires have indicated modding is, in many cases, a collaborative effort where mod developers from all over the world donate time and skills and work together on various aspects of production and development (Nieborg 2005; Postigo 2008).

The various kinds of inputs provided by mod developers can provide value to the developer firm and (extended) community at large through their—in many cases, freely shared—knowledge and labour contributions (Banks 2013). Free labour through value-adding practices balances somewhere in between paid and voluntary work (Hong and Chen 2013; Postigo 2007; Terranova 2000). The challenge of such 'precarious playbour' is the 'recognition of their status as creators of value for the industry and gamers alike, claiming their intellectual property rights and overcoming the ideological representation of modding as mere hobby' (Küchlich 2005: 7). In fact, mod developers operate in a firm-hosted community from which the developer firm continuously seeks to benefit, albeit by proxy (Prax 2016). Thus, firms regard mod development as attractive sources for free brand creation, extensions of the game's shelf-life, increased loyalty, innovation and recruitment, while users seem to be drawn by activities such as problem solving, hacking, self-expression and portfolio building (Behr 2007; Jeppesen 2004; Moody 2014).

Whereas both mod developers and developer firms actively appropriate and rework digital resources, it is typically only the developer firm that can claim full rights over their products and the firms have developed legal contracts outlining what can and cannot be done with the product; 'the consequence is that we are less and less a free culture, more and more a permission culture' (Lessig 2004: 8). Issues of artistic appropriation and fair use may have been dealt with in other media contexts such as music and film to 'balance the rights of original creators' rights of intellectual property with subsequent creators' rights to expressive re-imaginings of that original material', yet legal scholarship concerning games/3D environments has tended to concentrate on the underlying code rather than user experiences (Baldrica 2007: 684). The rights of mod developers tend to be bound by the firm's End-User License Agreement that typically denies any type of ownership and, as such, contributes to an unbalanced sketch of firm–user relationships in product development (Banks 2013; Humphreys 2008). The legal pay-off for user participation in development practices in games/3D environments remains pretty marginal in terms of legal protection and ownership rights associated with user creativity.

Within this context, one might wonder how mod developers perceive this 'industry gain' of the 'labour of love' they put in creation practices (in a romanticized picture of working) at night and in the wee hours of the morning within the confines of their homes. Who are all those 'you's' that are claimed to indulge in online cultural production? Without much systematic research readily available on user participation in an online context, the studies that have appeared present a rather bleak picture, indicating that a relatively small percentage of users are actual creators of, for example, blogs, upload videos, game mods (Burgess 2007; Li and Bernoff 2008; van Dijck 2009, 2013). The majority of users seem to consist of those who like to be entertained by reading, watching, and downloading content contributed by others. Research has also insufficiently addressed motivations for participation, which may be motivated by a communal desire associated with a shared enterprise or interest but may also be driven by individual needs or interests. Moreover, in the investigation of user participation no distinction tends to be made between users of firm-hosted and not-for-profit communities (cf. de Valck 2005; Schäfer 2008).

A rapidly growing body of scholarship can be detected in the evolving field of game-like environment research. So, what is known about users participating in the context of such environments? Multiple studies have suggested that gamers are wide and diverse, underpinned by differences in game genres and platforms—this contrary to a more stereotypical perception of gamers as isolated teenage males (Delwiche and Henderson 2013). One well-known taxonomy of virtual world players, albeit developed without statistical data, was developed by Bartle (1996), which distinguishes between achievers, socializers, explorers and killers. With Bartle's taxonomy in mind Yee's study (2006), developed a taxonomy of players based on MMORPG demographics, motivations and experiences. Insight was yielded into, among other things, the relationship between the avatar and the offline personality, playing with real life romantic partners, and economic profitability from digital sales. Yee's taxonomy has in turn laid the groundwork for an assessment of gamer motivations (Hou 2011; Greenberg et al. 2010; Tamborini et al. 2010; Williams et al. 2008), role-playing in online games (Williams et al. 2010), gender roles (Johnson 2013; Williams et al. 2009), age (Pearce 2008; De Schutter and Abeele 2010) and the dynamic between psychosocial well-being and online behaviour (Shen and Williams 2011).

Only a handful of studies have examined the motivations of players who develop modifications. Detected dimensions for participation include playing, hacking, researching, artistic work and cooperation (Sotamaa 2007). Similar findings can be found in Behr's work (2007) in which she interviewed fourteen modders of different mod communities, while adding the motivations of facing challenges and gaining recognition. In addition to motivations, she also considered usage patterns of the modding technology in terms of communication, behaviour, perceived social norms and restrictions. While showing similar motivational patterns, mod developers could be classified in terms of usage patterns as committed youngsters, experienced leaders, part-time modders and project-oriented modders.

With its focus on democratizing aspects of user creativity, or, in other words, social advancement through technological progress associated with Web 2.0, the user participation literature offers a good starting-point for the investigation of the firm-hosted 3D platform as a site of participatory culture. The review of existing literature shows that, in the context of this book, there are weaknesses in the theoretical, empirical and methodological approaches. One weakness is related to the apparent link between user participation and technological advancement. Too readily research tends to overestimate (or, 'hype') the creative capacities of users and their contributions to product development, while aspects of (such as variations in) the design and use of technologies (e.g., software routines, toolkits) tend to be under exposed, or even absent from many discussions. Moreover, scholars have been quick to relate this kind of social progress through user participation to the organization of the (digital) media or content industry, where some kind of shift in the power relations between firms and users seems to be implied rather than systematically investigated. Also, insufficient attention has been given to the ways users may participate on the firm-hosted platform (in contrast to not-for-profit platforms), what they may contribute, and how and with what frequency they may interact with others. On a similar note, a blind spot seems to have developed concerning the role of the firm, directing our attention from 'firms as producers' to 'firms as platform (or, service) providers' coinciding with a shift in legal contracts, and which, arguably, underpins the extent of user participation.

As this book aims to highlight the unfolding dynamics between the various participants involved in product development, rather than concentrating only on the roles of users-as-participants on the firm-hosted 3D platform, the investigation is supported by themes within the communities of practice tradition and the user-centred innovation literature. In doing so, this work seeks to address some of the weaknesses of the user participation literature underpinning the identification and analysis of the constituents involved in the development and organization of product development across firm boundaries. These literatures are used to draw particular attention to interdependencies developing between the firm, users and technologies on the firm-hosted platform, thereby illuminating the growing significance of users in knowledge production and innovation associated with the emerging knowledge-based economy.

2.3   The Wisdom of the Firm

Firms have come to rely on properties of online communities such as social networking sites to acquire, engage and retain users. Communities are viewed as opportunities for firms and users to meet, where knowledge and information can be generated and exchanged and transactions executed. More specifically, the rise of user creativity is said to downplay professional expertise associated with a closed and proprietary-based understanding of the firm, favouring the growth of knowledge associated with open networks encompassing all participants, across firm boundaries. These converging firm-user dynamics occurring in communities, or networks, of practice draw attention to the importance of the role of knowledge in social and economic development stressing the 'need to continuously harness new technologies and processes to develop knowledge societies that are people-centred, inclusive and development oriented' (UNESCO 2007: 1).

Since the early 1990s, a substantial literature can be identified that focusses on the role of communities in knowledge production and innovation that, in various research contexts, is informed by concepts such as epistemic communities (Haas 1992), communities of consumption (Kozinets 1999), and communities of practice (Lave and Wenger 1991). In particular, communities of practice (CoP) theory is useful here for its application in management and organization studies drawing attention to a knowledge-based view of the firm built around communities (cf. Grant 1996). Lave and Wenger (1991) originally developed the notion of CoP to understand learning as a situated activity outside the formal education system. In five accounts of apprenticeship in rather small and tight-knit communities of such as Mayan midwives in Yucatan and US supermarket butchers, they have provided an understanding of learning as a social process encapsulating a group of people engaged in a shared practice.

This learning model involves a process of 'legitimate peripheral participation' (LPP) that highlights an interdependent relationship between being a newcomer and being an insider in the community. LPP draws attention to ways in which outsiders become new participants and learn (preferred) ways of participating, reframing participants' ways of thinking, interests, shared practices and identities and so forth binding the community. Thus, LPP provides insight into the process whereby newcomers entering a community learn practices from the old timers. This process involves some sort of contribution from the apprentice to the community and when s/he masters these peripheral practices an increase in her/his legitimacy can mean (slowly) progressing inwards from the periphery to becoming an established and fully participating member. For example, peripheral participation can be detected in World of Warcraft (Blizzard Entertainment) and is built into the character's beginner's level enculturating them into the community by simple quests and instructions, while others act as mentors guiding them into the game's social functions (Lau 2005).

This movement from the 'outside towards the centre' through becoming embedded in the practices of the (core) community points to questions of power. Access and transparency are hereby relevant in order to be able to become a full member. Certain authority levels exist that explicitly or tacitly permit or refuse someone's membership status, thus, achieving the status of legitimate apprentice does not automatically mean the right to move towards participation in the more advanced practices of the community. Understanding power in terms of acceptance and denial seems somewhat limited, however. For example, Berdou (2011) has shown that in many Free and Open Source (F/OS) communities inequality remains an issue after a newcomer has been accepted as a member. She argues that the open and fluid character of the community may widen the idea of membership yet with many formal and informal rules in place a sense of hierarchy may become re-established. Moreover, not every newcomer may have a desire to move to centre stage and achieve full participation. Some members that are considered to contribute peripheral practices such as administrative tasks may not necessarily be interested in becoming core programmers. This seems to challenge the fairly independent and unconnected CoP perspective, warranting a more complex and multilevelled outlook of CoP in the context of variances in user participation in software development at the invitation of modern-day firms

In an organizational context the CoP perspective has been applied with particular attention to knowledge sharing within and across CoP, highlighting the notion 'constellations of interconnected practices' (Wenger 1998) and 'networks of practice' (NoP) (Brown and Duguid 2001). The former stresses the configuration of diverse but related CoP that, for instance, emerge across teams or firm boundaries, while the NoP encapsulates multiple and interconnected forms of social alignment stressing the flow of varying yet equally important degrees of proximity of information or relationships constituted by loose epistemic groups. The terms network and community are not clear-cut and have received much scholarly attention yet, generally, it can be said that a network refers to (somewhat) loosely coupled groups of members that may never come across one another (cf. de Valck 2005; Feenberg and Bakardjieva 2004; Rheingold 1993; Wenger 1998). It seems therefore that NoP is more appropriate in the context of web-based applications such as forums, F/OS projects and 3D environments, although both NoP and CoP have been widely (often, interchangeably) applied. This book builds on the perspective of a constellation of practices that are networked in principle, accentuating different dynamics and interdependencies among networked CoP (NCoP) where the fluid boundaries between the different practices are constantly fine-tuned.

The importance of communities as facilitators of knowledge production, sharing and application has, especially since the mid-1990s, coincided with a move in theories of the firm towards a knowledge-based view of the firm (Grant 1996).[3] In this knowledge-based view, the production of knowledge is understood as the most important resource, or activity, of the firm and is a key source for competitive advantage (Nonaka 1991; Teece 1998). The success of firms or individuals is reflected in their capability to learn associated with the generation, exchange, and utilization of new knowledge, competence and skills; it can be said that the firm or individuals generate wealth in proportion to their capacity to learn and share their creations (Foray 2004; cf. 'learning economy' in Lundvall 1996).

Notwithstanding long-standing debates that have sought to define knowledge, here, knowledge is understood as a (cognitive) capability. Knowledge can be defined by 'what we know' (Polanyi 1969), information on the other hand, is about expressing what we know such as through the written word or photographs. Therefore, the reproduction of knowledge can be said to concern learning, while the reproduction of information deals with duplication (cf. Foray and Steinmueller 2003). And whereas the marginal costs of information reproduction are close to zero, learning relies on a 'master-apprentice system [...] or on interpersonal transactions among members of the same profession or community of practice' (Foray 2004: 4). For example, using a cognitive ethnography methodology Steinkuehler (2005) selected a single unremarkable utterance of reoccurring collaborative practice in the virtual world Lineage (NCsoft) and used functional linguistics to yield insight into the nature of a given practice in-world, and the way language-in-use was situated and tied to the larger community marking membership within that community.

This draws attention to an aspect of transferability of knowledge, which effectively underlies the sustainability of competitive advantage (Kakihara and Sørensen 2002). In this view, knowledge rather than being captured can be demonstrated through people's expressions and practices in relation to a social learning context of the NCoP. A knowledge-based view of the firm therefore recognizes communities as effective organizational means that enable and facilitate complex (tacit) knowledge sharing. Communities have been documented to support (voluntary) knowledge sharing, inform the development of relationships, nurture new knowledge, stimulate innovation and share knowledge within and across firm boundaries (Antorini 2007; Davenport et al. 2006; Lueg 2003; Prahalad and Krishnan 2008; Wenger 1998). Attention has been drawn to the growing importance of networked sites, or communities, as repositories of knowledge (and innovation) advocating a view of learning that is profoundly linked to the conditions within which it is learned. The knowledge-based perspective understands learning as an interactive process where knowledge is a collective asset dispersed among networked firms and individuals, while enhancing competences of both. Through these networked communities users are seen to engage in various practices and exchange information, providing a basis for the firm's ability to know and learn, highlighting users as part of the firm's dynamic knowledge base. More specifically, where the firm actively seeks input from its users as external knowledge sources, firm boundaries can be defined by its knowledge base rather than by the firm's production function alone (cf. Foray 2004).

When firms open up to inflows and outflows of knowledge for the advancement of product or platform development several challenges lie ahead such as attracting and motivating users to participate, allocating and coordinating inputs and outputs between the firm and the user base, and accessing, filtering and incorporating user contributions. The investigation into the underlying dynamics of the production, distribution and application of knowledge and its impact on economic development has been wide and diverse and with different theoretical positions and contributions clear-cut lines and robust constructs for further investigation are not easily distilled. For example, a substantial literature has concentrated on issues such as the accessibility and diffusion of knowledge yet has tended to bypass the organization of processes by which firms manage to stimulate, access and convert (external) knowledge into specific competences and capabilities (cf. Washida et al. 2006). Also, the adoption of CoP in a commercial setting raises an important question about characterization, highlighting the community as a structure of interdependence marked by relations of a minimal hierarchy and organizational heterogeneity associated with bottom-up and egalitarian accounts of power (Powell 1990). However, the community associated with the firm tends to be brought about by completing tasks and is generally related to financial rewards. Lastly, with the 'explosion of information' associated with the proliferation of digital technologies underpinned by concepts such as the 'networked information economy' and the 'learning economy', it may become increasingly difficult for firms to recognize and keep up with significant trends that may confer sustainable competitive advantage.

2.4   Toolkits for User Innovation

Innovation as a field of research has emerged since the 1960s and focuses on the sources of innovation and information, thereby recognizing that some of the most important new products and processes have been developed by user firms and end users (Bogers et al. 2016; Freeman 1991; von Hippel 2005).[4] Given the scope of this book, the focus is on innovation by users or consumers and focuses on issues that arise from the tension between need information (generated by users) and solution information (generally originated by developer firm), known as information stickiness. In this view, successful product or platform development is about information costs, where the firm looks to reduce the acquisition of reliable needs information in administering a product tailored to users' specific needs, while at the same time, to improve the knowledge base of the whole firm (van der Graaf 2012a). Firms and users are said to know different things, resulting in the development of different types of innovations: firm-related innovation is based on known needs while functionality is stressed by user-driven innovation (von Hippel 1994). It can be expensive though to move information from one site to another.[5] User needs can also change on product usage and can devalue outdated user information stored by the developer firm (Jeppesen 2004).

Information stickiness, however, can be reduced. In particular, new contributions or modifications can be developed without the transfer of sticky information from users if they perform particular design tasks. Firm-provided toolkits have been shown to assist in this practice of systematically outsourcing certain design and innovation tasks from the locus of the firm to users. Toolkits tend to lower the threshold by enabling and facilitating user participation in development practices, supporting them to develop according to their own needs (Piller and Walcher 2006; von Hippel and Katz 2002). As a result, the development practice is repartitioned into sub-tasks between the firm and users, co-locating 'problem solving tasks with sticky need-related information in the consumer setting', which draws attention to modularity (Jeppesen 2004: 17). A modular system can be understood as, 'a nearly decomposable system that preserves the possibility of cooperation by adopting a common interface. The common interface enables, but also governs and disciplines, the communication among subsystems' (Langlois and Garzarelli 2006: 9).

Modularity as a development strategy can offer a number of advantages, such as mitigating the task of coordination, allowing upgrading per module, or throughout the product life cycle (particularly associated with the degree of standardization of the interface), and reducing production costs and time (e.g., different modules can be simultaneously developed and tapped into local knowledge) (Gawer 2009; Evans 2010; cf. 'collective intelligence' in Lévy 1997). Several disadvantages of modularity include a possible decrease, especially in the short term, in overall product performance and, in comparison to non-compound systems, a modular system is more complex and, hence, a more thorough understanding of connections between modules is necessary in order to develop the system (Langlois and Robertson 1992; Ulrich 1995). The deployment of toolkits in this context provides users with different modalities in design possibilities, ranging from having a very simple scope ('low-end') such as selecting between various options like size and colour, to allowing them to come up with new products ('high-end') (Thomke and von Hippel 2002). The more basic type of toolkit is typically used to exploit mature markets, while the more advanced kind tends to be used in the exploration of new and/or opportunities for products and services. Furthermore, it has been shown that high-end (or, expert) toolkits tend to pose a greater challenge to users and, consequently, demand a more advanced skill level, while low-end toolkits can be used by nearly any user (see key attributes of successful toolkits for the firm, in von Hippel 2005).

The introduction chapter highlighted that, especially, FPS, virtual worlds and 3D collaborative platforms can be equipped with a toolkit enabling and guiding mod developers top unlock (some of) the capabilities of the software's core. What can we learn from the use of toolkits in the game-like software industries? In their study on The Sims (Maxis) Prügl and Schreier (2006) sought to go beyond a solution-based perspective on the utilization of toolkits by investigating how users actually manage this invitation to participate. By examining types of innovative practices, the handling of firm-provided toolkits and peer relevance of user-generated outputs, they found that users were not satisfied with the firm-provided tools; 'Instead, they tried to surpass the limits of the design freedom provided in firm-constructed toolkits by employing tools from related fields and by expanding the scope of existing tools or even creating their own toolkits. [...] different types of users employ different types of tools, which in turn lead to different types of innovation activities' (Prügl and Schreier 2006: 247). Thus, a so-called 'firm-constructed design limit' can be detected that constructs the space for user-driven innovation (Jeppesen 2004; cf. 'solution space' in von Hippel 2001; 'third place' in Jenkins 2006). Moreover, this practice seems to reveal a tension between firm strategy and user communities that the firm harnesses by providing tools that shape the basis of a 'community-of-practices' as a solution and meeting place that prompt users' learning and innovation practices (Jeppesen and Molin 2003).

From this perspective, the user-centred innovation framework can be said to position mod development underpinned by the qualities of the toolkit, within the established, capital-intensive boundaries of the proprietary technology of the developer firm (cf. Nieborg and van der Graaf 2008). This draws attention to the issue of generativity that Zittrain (2008: 70) has defined as 'a system's capacity to produce unanticipated change through unfiltered contributions from broad and varied audiences'. In this context, Zittrain (2008) has argued that the qualities that gave rise to the success of the Internet now seem to be losing strength while pointing to a resurgence of bundled hardware and software produced and controlled by one firm. Nowadays, it seems less easy for users to modify Internet-centred platform products and services in contrast to the firm and/or selected partners.

Another issue concerns the application of user toolkits in support of the firm's competitive position. Research has primarily concentrated on the short term of toolkits for user-centred innovation, but what happens when savvy users learn the 'trade' and develop a competitive relationship with the developer firm? Also, not much systematic attention has been given to heterogeneous user needs and characteristics in relation to the supply of different toolkits and the role of firm support to sustain the quality of user-generated contributions for application in the firm (and community) (Jeppesen 2004) warranting the question: what kind of innovating practices do users participate in? Moreover, who are these users, and what are their motivations?

Users have been shown to participate in innovation-related practices in areas such as industrial (von Hippel 1976; Lettl et al. 2006), consumer (Lüthje 2004) and information (Frederiksen 2006) products. Also, an increased focus on 'community-based innovation' can be observed (Antorini 2007; Jeppesen 2004). The underlying idea is that users inspire, assist and collaborate with each other in innovation practices. These innovation communities are 'nodes' encompassing people and/or firms supported by information transfer links such as face-to-face and electronic (von Hippel 2005). With a focus on a community based perspective on shared interests and innovation-related practices, this outlook is quite similar to the CoP perspective. Research into innovation communities has indicated that users tend to rely mostly on each other for innovation-related information than, for example, on web site resources (Lüthje 2004); and users in several sports communities collaborate, provide and receive quality innovation-related assistance supporting the innovation process, yet they find themselves in a competitive setting the members share less (or nothing) (Franke and Shah 2003). Also, F/OS projects have been studied in this context, for example, in terms of the cost of joining, contributing and specialization of newcomers in developer communities (von Krogh et al. 2003), and the managerial challenges encountered when software firms seek to interrelate with F/OS communities for purposes such as value generation (Dahlander and Magnusson 2005).

Not every user who innovates is the next Gabe Newell (Valve), or Mark Zuckerberg (Facebook) for that matter. Von Hippel (1986) has shown that a small group of users tends to be ahead on market trends prior to adoption by the masses. Moreover, they can point out what they consider to be flaws (in terms of needs and solutions) from which the firm can learn, increasing the likelihood of a successful release in the mainstream market (Lilien et al. 2002). These users who find themselves at the leading edge of soon-to-be-trends, 'expect attractive innovation-related benefits from a solution and so are motivated to innovate, and [...] they experience the need for a given innovation earlier than the majority of the target market' (Jeppesen 2004: 14). This so-called 'lead user' construct, coined by von Hippel (1986), consists of the variables 'ahead of the market', 'level of expected benefit' and 'level of innovation'.[6] It tends to be empirically tested on the basis of dividing users into dichotomous 'lead user' versus 'non-lead user' categories (see, sports communities in Franke and Shah 2003; mod communities in Jeppesen and Molin 2003).

Morrison et al. (2004) have sought to validate the lead user construct by introducing the variable 'leading edge status' (LES) that was tested on a sample of innovating and non-innovating users of Australian libraries. Among other things, they found that the distribution of LES was unimodal indicating that a dichotomous understanding of lead users versus others is somewhat arbitrary and 'throws away valuable information' (Morrison et al. 2004: 361; cf. Franke and von Hippel 2002). Yet, a more nuanced approach towards the empirical investigation of characteristics among different users as innovators fulfilling different roles associated with various levels of involvement has remained largely unexplored. Furthermore, an overly strong reliance on personal experiences/needs of lead users may dampen successful mainstream adaptation because of certain differences between lead users and mass users (Watts and Dodds 2007). However, in the case of niche markets, the experience/needs of lead users can be very helpful because they tend to have quite similar attributes to within-firm developers (Kujala 2003).

Why do users participate in innovation practices? Research has shown that users engage in innovations if their use benefits exceed their costs (von Hippel 2005). Thus, users tend to innovate because they seek to satisfy their own needs. In general, however, research has tended to examine motives independently, highlighting a number of intrinsic motivations such as enjoyment, learning and the process of participation, and extrinsic benefits such as firm and peer recognition and career advancement (Antorini 2007; Jeppesen and Frederiksen 2006; Lakhani and Wolf 2003; Shah 2006). Research has also shown that users, in the case of freely shared developments, can out-compete closed, firm-innovators because they seem to be able to gather more capable and diverse participants than firms can, and when developments are freely shared all participants can share and use the best contribution any participating user has developed (Baldwin et al. 2006). This seems to present opportunities for mod developers to commercialize their contributions and benefit beyond mere personal use yet substantial evidence of entrepreneurship is lacking and contested (von Hippel 1976, 1988; Lettl et al. 2006; Shah 2000). It has been suggested, however, that personal characteristics and information possessed by the entrepreneur may account for starting up a firm and that the likelihood of user entrepreneurship may relate to opportunity costs (Shah and Tripsas 2004). Furthermore, open product design, modular product architecture and stage in the industry life cycle can positively advance the commercialization of user-driven innovations (cf. Hienerth 2004).

2.5   Conclusion: Digital Innovation Platforms

The Internet connects people across time and space by means of accessible and scalable communication channels, allowing one-to-one, one-to-many and many-to-many interactions. Facilitated by diverse platforms that underlie countless new connections between people that gather, participate, create and form publics, strategies can be detected addressing various user groups to satisfy manifold niches of sociality and creativity as well as competition (Feenberg 2009). In fact, the term platform has become the dominant concept for digital or so-called platform companies to describe their role in the market and their services towards their users. In media studies, for example, the term is utilized to describe the 'discursive work' it undertakes (Gillespie 2010: 348) and how software is shaping participation and connectivity (Bucher 2012; Hands 2013; Langlois et al. 2009; van Dijck 2013). Many definitions can be detected highlighting the term's various connotations. In terms of its medium specificity a platform can be appreciated for its specific technological architecture and ontological distinctiveness in terms of its 'programmability' (Evans et al. 2006; Helmond 2015; Rogers 2013). A digital platform can be defined as 'a reconfigurable base of compatible components on which firms and users build applications. Applications share the general purpose components, thereby exploiting increasing returns at an industry wide level' (Bresnahan and Greenstein 2014: 475). This understanding explicitly opens up sites that are changeable (programmable) for third parties or stakeholders through software interfaces, for instance Application Programming Interfaces (API). Mansell (2016) rightfully points out, however, that this definition fails to address how platform companies harvest social computing and respective implications for citizens. Bogost and Montfort (2009) urge for technical rigor in understanding the relationship between technical specifics and culture. Somewhat contrasting, Gillespie (2010) developed a more conceptual understanding of the term by drawing out its computational, political, figurative and architectural features so as to facilitate platforms to bring various actors together, thereby emphasizing the participatory and economic aspects of platforms. Here, the computational version appeals to developers, while the others are more meaningful to users, advertisers, clients and so forth.

This description resonates with the economics and management literature associated with 'multisided markets' in which a platform enables
interactions between two or more distinct parties (Rochet and Tirole
2003). Users, advertisers and third-party developers are, for example,
brought together by Facebook, benefiting from network effects as they
use it (Hagiu 2014). More specifically, platforms have often been
approached from two distinct perspectives, that is, 'platforms as markets'
or 'platforms as modular technological architectures' (Gawer 2014).
Increasingly work is being done to join these perspectives and which 'can
extend analyses of concrete configurations of power and identify control
points, structural dynamics and crucial resources for argumentation'
(Rieder and Sire 2014: 208).

Accepting this outlook on platforms, this book examines how the
firm-user dynamics are played out by looking at how the modular technical architecture of the collaborative 3D platform connects to and
enacts its socio-economic model underpinned by emerging norms and
values (cf. 'platform politics' in Bucher 2013; Hands 2013; Langlois and
Elmer 2013; Puschmann and Burgess 2013; van Dijck 2013). In doing
so, the emerging reconfiguration of the digital platform (and business
models) vis-à-vis user creativity becomes apparent transforming the
roles, identities and politics of content creation and sharing on the
Internet, underpinned or paralleled by a seeming evolution of platform
objectives. YouTube (2005), for example, was at its origins a platform
catering to a community of video creators and has evolved to one that
mostly caters to users interested in merely consuming content (Burgess
et al. 2009). Moreover, videos on YouTube are increasingly produced and
owned by companies that then hold copyright over user-generated content. This has resulted in discussions about monetization practices of
Google, particularly regarding ownership and exploitation, pointing to
the formalization, or regulation of 'free' labour (cf. Postigo 2014). This
practice is called 'platform mainstreaming' (van der Graaf and Fisher
2017).

In order to understand this phenomenon better, this book adopts the
perspective that user participation on the firm-hosted 3D platform is an
emerging site of participatory culture and indicative of a blending
together of sociality and market and, in this capacity, may generate

considerable market value. This view offers the opportunity to build on the concept of 'connective market' by examining non-market dynamics connected with user participation (which tends to be associated with the idea of free labour) in the commercial setting of the firm-hosted platform.

User participation is investigated as a dynamic process evoked in a context and particular organization of the roles of different groups of contributors (including the developer firm and individuals) that are networked in a constellation of practices underlying product development with the aim of highlighting the interdependencies developing between the firm, users and technologies on the firm-hosted 3D platform (Wadell et al. 2013; Lee 2015). More specifically, the way modular aspects associated with the nature of the product/platform coordinate (often, temporary) work practices between the developer firm and users demands attention. As pointed out, inviting users to participate, connect and 'co-create', a shift can be detected from a more closed production and innovation model to a more open, distributed and modular model. This calls into question the mechanisms of work coordination, and which arguably, is associated with organizing work on a (seemingly) temporary basis, thereby highlighting the nature of the product life cycle. A temporary organization design is flexible, discontinuous and ephemeral (van der Graaf 2012b). It is also entangled with a social context instead of lines of authority that provide 'expertise, reputation, and legitimization' as key resources (Grabher 2004: 1492; Lave and Wenger 1991). This 'coordinate and cultivate' style of management (contrary to command and control) entails questions on how work(ers) can be organized efficiently such as in the context of the platform (Bechky 2006; Malone 2004). There is, however, a lack of empirical studies about work dynamics, performance and organization in minimal hierarchy, minimal formal structure firms, as well as the impacts on workers.

In this book, therefore, attention is given to role structures so as to yield insight into emergent practices underpinning coordination processes of transient work conditions, thereby highlighting how heterogeneous knowledge sources can coordinate work as gatekeepers of information and value flows between the different stakeholders associated with emerging norms of participation and values of creativity (D'Adderio 2002; cf. 'multisided market strategy' and 'platform leadership'; Ballon and

Van Heesvelde 2011; Gawer 2009). Variations in several participation patterns among contributing users (operationalized through the 'design capabilities', see Chap. 3) are empirically investigated to come to a more robust insight into differences in creative capacities among user contributions and the implications for the platform development process across firm boundaries.

By drawing on insights from the toolkits for user innovation perspective, this work investigates how user participation is embedded in commerce on the firm-hosted platform, thereby directing particular attention to technical and artificial qualities of the toolkit (operationalized through the wider 'design space', see Chap. 4) that underpin the use and design of the platform. The supply of different toolkits is also examined in connection with variations in the characteristics of users such as different roles and degrees of involvement; so as to elaborate firm-user interactions in terms of the role of the firm-as-provider and the ways users may participate, what they may contribute, and how and with what frequency they may interact with others on the firm-hosted platform (in contrast to not-for-profit platforms), which is further expected to yield insight the commercialization of user contributions and the implications for the firm's competitive position. Thus, firm-provided user toolkits are empirically investigated to come to a more robust understanding of the organization of firm–user relationships with particular attention to variations in participation patterns and functionalities of the design space and implications for platform development.

From this perspective, the firm-hosted platform as a site of participatory culture underpinning platform development, is investigated as a repository of knowledge (that can be demonstrated) mobilizing the investigation of learning as an interactive process between the developer firm and users (operationalized through 'learning by design', see Chap. 5), which is associated with the emerging knowledge-based economy. This includes the strategy of the developer firm to engage users in creation and sharing practices on the firm-hosted platform providing a basis for the firm's ability to know and learn. In this examination, this book considers the organization of processes by which the developer firm seeks to enable, facilitate and manage (external) knowledge into specific competences and capabilities, and relate available information to various aspects of learning opportunities, for which the implications are also considered for the subsidiary communities of practice perspective.

In doing so, a more robust understanding of the development and organization of firm–user relationships that underlies the integration of user participation into mainstream business and the implications for platform development can be revealed, at a significant moment in time.

Notes

1. This influential work draws attention to the multifaceted nature of people's relationships with media investigated in audience research, in particular, the branch of audience reception research that concerns the interpretative analysis of audience reception. A range of research has occurred especially focusing on interaction between text and reception underlying extensive debates concerning active-passive and homogenous-divergent perceptions of audiences (Fiske 1987; Hall 1980; Morley 1993). From this perspective, Livingstone (2007: 19–20) concludes that 'research has clearly shown that audiences are plural in their decodings, that their cultural context matters and that they cannot be presumed to agree with textual analysis […]' and, in order to 'elucidate when and where and under what circumstances different kinds of sense-making occur', more research is needed into the many parameters underpinned by textual and social determinations. The concept of participatory culture has indeed sought to distinguish between active media spectatorship as user participation in online cultural production and a kind of consumer culture emphasizing the mere consumption of corporate media content (Jenkins 1992, 2006). In this view, users are migratory, socially connected, and resistant, describing a 'collective intelligence' where users have more control over the flow of information brought to them by firms. Involvement in a participatory culture can therefore range from community membership based on shared interests, to active engagement in practices such as collaborative problem solving and digital development. This implies that all members may contribute according to their own desire, needs, and skills to do so.
2. The Internet for example, is a site where cultural, social, and economic value has been produced and obtained, facilitated by platforms from Geocities, MySpace, to Facebook, and, arguably, co-evolved with people

who use them (Burgess and Woodford 2015; Gitelman 2006; Helmond 2015; Sapnar Ankerson 2015). Different degrees of user engagement have been identified in multiple studies, ranging from low-level inputs (such as a 'like' on Facebook) to high levels of participation or creativity (the generation of elaborate code to produce total conversion modifications of games a la Defense of the Ancients (DOTA)).

3. This perspective, arguably, succeeded a 'first-generation' knowledge-centric view of the firm that was information technology and systems based suggesting that there has been a shift from collecting knowledge to perspectives on connecting people (Huysman and de Wit 2004).

4. The term innovation, in this book, is broadly viewed as aspirational, interactive, and integrative entailing ways of seeing and doing ideas, objects, and practices perceived as new by an adopting unit (Rogers 2003). Specifically, the term refers to (production) practices concerning user participation/creativity without regard to the nuances in existing literature about the relationships between innovation, creativity and/or production or economists' conceptions of innovation, creativity, and knowledge. Innovation also concerns the organization of firm-user interactions shaping and maintaining the firm-hosted platform rather than highlighting the role of the individual or specific points of within-firm innovation (cf. Fontana and Sørensen 2005).

5. For example, tacit information tends to be expensive because it is typically accessed and acquired through apprenticeship systems (von Hippel 2005).

6. Various mechanisms can be used to identify lead users such as pyramiding, specialized events, tracking of download figures, and user communications on web sites (Frederiksen 2006; Prügl and Schreier 2006; von Hippel 2005).

References

Allen, D., Bailey, M., Carpentier, N., Fenton, N., Jenkins, H., Lothian, A., Linchuan Qui, J., Schaefer, M. T., & Srinivasan, R. (2014). Participations: Dialogues on the Participatory Promise of Contemporary Culture and Politics. *International Journal of Communication, 8*, 1129–1151.

Antorini, Y. M. (2007). *Brand Community Innovation: An Intrinsic Case Study of the Adult Fans of LEGO Community*. Unpublished Ph.D., Copenhagen Business School, Copenhagen.

Armstrong, M. (2006). Competition in Two-Sided Markets. *The Rand Journal of Economics, 37*(3), 668–691. doi:10.1111/j.1756-2171.2006.tb00037.x.

Baldrica, J. (2007). Mod as Heck: Frameworks for Examining Ownership Rights in User-Contributed Content to Videogames, and a More Principled Evaluation of Expressive Appropriation in User-Modified Videogame Projects. *Minnesota Journal of Law, Science & Technology, 8*(2), 681–713.

Baldwin, C., Hienerth, C., & von Hippel, E. (2006). *How User Innovations Become Commercial Products: A Theoretical Investigation and Case Study.* Retrieved August 9, 2008, from http://www.people.hbs.edu/cbaldwin/DR2/BHVRODEOKayakHBSWPv2.pdf

Ballon, P. (2009). *Platform Types and Gatekeeper Roles: The Case of the Mobile Communications Industry.* Presented at the Summer Conference on CBS-Copenhagen Business School, Denmark.

Ballon, P., & Van Heesvelde, E. (2011, May 31–June 2). *Platform Markets and Regulatory Concerns in the ICT Industry: A Taxonomic Approach.* Extended Abstract for the Conference on "Platform Markets: Regulation and Competition Policy", Mannheim.

Ballon, P., Walravens, N., Spedalieri, A., & Venezia, C. (2010). The Reconfiguration of Mobile Service Provision: Towards Platform Business Models. In M. Falch & J. Markendahl (Eds.), *Promoting New Telecom Infrastructures: Markets, Policies and Pricing* (pp. 197–216). Cheltenham/Northampton: Edward Elgar.

Banks, J. (2013). *Co-creating Videogames.* London: Bloomsbury Academic.

Bartle, R. (1996). Hearts, Clubs, Diamonds, Spades: Players Who Suit MUDs. Retrieved March 11, 2017, from http://www.mud.co.uk/richard/hcds.htm

Bechky, B. (2006). Gaffers, Gofers, and Grips: Role-Based Coordination in Temporary Organizations. *Organization Science, 17*(1), 3–21.

Behr, K.-M. (2007). *The Development of Computer Game Modifications: Creators of Games Content Explored.* Paper Presented at the 58th International Communication Association, San Francisco.

Benkler, Y. (2006). *The Wealth of Networks: How Social Production Transforms Markets and Freedom.* New Haven: Yale University Press.

Berdou, E. (2011). *Organization in Open Source Communities: At the Crossroads of the Gift and Market Economies.* London: Routledge.

Bilton, C. (2007). *Management and Creativity: From Creative Industries to Creative Management.* Oxford: Blackwell Publishing.

Bogers, M., Zobel, A.-K., Afuah, A., Almirall, E., Brunswicker, S., Dahlander, L., Frederiksen, L., Gawer, A., Gruber, M., Haefliger, S., Hagedoorn, J.,

Hilgers, D., Laursen, K., Magnusson, M., Majchrzak, A., McCarthy, I., Moeslein, K., Nambisan, S., Piller, F., Radziwon, A., Rossi-Lamastra, C., Sims, J., & Ter Wal, A. (2016). The Open Innovation Research Landscape: Established Perspectives and Emerging Themes Across Different Levels of Analysis. *Industry and Innovation, 24*(1), 8–40.

Bogost, I., & Montfort, N. (2009). Platform Studies: Frequently Questioned Answers. *Digital Arts and Culture.* Retrieved from http://escholarship.org/uc/item/01r0k9br.pdf

Bresnahan, T., & Greenstein, S. (2014). Mobile Computing: The Next Platform Rivalry. *American Economic Review, 104*(5), 475–480.

Brown, J. S., & Duguid, P. (2001). Knowledge and Organization: A Social-Practice Perspective. *Organization Science, 12*(2), 198–213.

Bruns, A. (2008). *Blogs, Wikipedia, Second Life, and Beyond: From Production to Produsage.* New York: Peter Lang.

Bucher, T. (2012). *Programmed Sociality: A Software Studies Perspective on Social Networking Sites.* Doctoral Dissertation, University of Oslo, Oslo.

Bucher, T. (2013). Objects of Intense Feeling: The Case of the Twitter API. *Computational Culture, 3.* Retrieved from http://computationalculture.net/article/objects-of-intense-feeling-the-case-of-the-twitter-api

Burgess, J. (2007). *Vernacular Creativity and New Media.* Unpublished Ph.D., Queensland University of Technology, Queensland.

Burgess, J., & Woodford, D. (2015). Content Creation and Curation. In R. Mansell & P. H. Ang (Eds.), *The International Encyclopedia of Digital Communication and Society, Wiley Blackwell-ICA Encyclopedias of Communication* (pp. 88–94). Malden and Oxford: Wiley-Blackwell.

Burgess, J., Green, J., Jenkins, H., & Hartley, J. (2009). *YouTube: Online Video and Participatory Culture.* Cambridge: Polity.

D'Adderio, L. (2002). *Inside the Virtual Product: The Influence of Integrated Software Systems on Organisational Knowledge Dynamics.* Unpublished Ph.D., University of Sussex.

Dahlander, L., & Magnusson, M. (2005). Relationships Between Open Source Software Companies and Communities: Observations from Nordic Firms. *Research Policy, 34,* 481–493.

Davenport, T., Leibold, M., & Voelpel, S. (2006). *Strategic Management in the Innovation Economy: Strategy Approaches and Tools for Dynamic Innovation Capabilities.* Erlangen: Publicis-Wiley.

De Schutter, B., & Abeele, V. (2010). Designing Meaningful Play Within the Psychosocial Context of Older Adults. In *Proceedings of the 3rd International*

Conference on Fun and Games (Fun and Games '10) (pp. 84–93). New York: ACM. doi:10.1145/1823818. 1823827.

de Valck, K. (2005). *Virtual Communities of Consumption: Networks of Consumer Knowledge and Companionship.* Unpublished Ph.D., Erasmus University Rotterdam, Rotterdam.

Delwiche, A., & Henderson, J. (2013). The Players They Are A-Changin': The Rise of Older MMO Gamers. *Journal of Broadcasting & Electronic Media, 57*(2), 205–233.

Deuze, M., Martin, C. B., & Allen, C. (2007). The Professional Identity of Gameworkers. *Convergence: The International Journal of Research into New Media Technologies, 13*(4), 335–353.

Evans, D. (2010). *Essays on the Economics of Two-Sided Markets: Economics, Antitrust and Strategy.* http://papers.ssrn.com/sol3/papers.cfm?abstract_id=1714254

Evans, D. S., Hagiu, A., & Schmalensee, R. (2006). *Invisible Engines: How Software Platforms Drive Innovation and Transform Industries.* Cambridge: MIT Press.

Feenberg, A. (2009). Critical Theory of Communication Technology: Introduction to the Special Section. *The Information Society, 25*(2), 77–83. doi:10.1080/01972240802701536.

Feenberg, A., & Bakardjieva, M. (2004). Virtual Community: No 'Killer Implication'. *New Media & Society, 6*(1), 37–43.

Fiske, J. (1987). *Television Culture.* London: Methuen.

Fontana, E. R., & Sørensen, C. (2005). From Idea to Blah! Understanding Mobile Services Development as Interactive. *Journal of Information Systems and Technology Management, 2*(2), 101–120.

Foray, D. (2004). *The Economics of Knowledge.* Cambridge, MA: MIT Press.

Foray, D., & Steinmueller, W. (2003). The Economics of Knowledge Reproduction by Inscription. *Industrial and Corporate Change, 12*(2), 299–319.

Franke, N., & Shah, S. (2003). How Communities Support Innovative Activities: An Exploration of Assistance and Sharing Among End-Users. *Research Policy, 32*, 157–178.

Franke, N., & von Hippel, E. (2002). Satisfying Heterogeneous User Needs via Innovation Toolkits: The Case of Apache Security Software. *Research Policy, 32*(7), 1199–1215. doi:10.1016/S0048-7333(03)00049-0.

Frederiksen, L. (2006). *User Communication Driving Firm Innovation: A communication Patterns Perspective on Personal Attributes and Communication Types in an Online User Community.* Retrieved July 16, 2007, from http://www2.druid.dk/conferences/viewpaper.php?id=540&cf=8

Freeman, C. (1991). Networks of Innovators: A Synthesis of Research Issues. *Research Policy, 20,* 499–514.

Gawer, A. (Ed.). (2009). *Platforms, Markets and Innovation.* Cheltenham/ Northampton: Edward Elgar.

Gawer, A. (2014). Bridging Differing Perspectives on Technological Platforms: Toward An Integrative Framework. *Research Policy, 43,* 1239–1249. doi:10.1016/j.respol.2014.03.006.

Gillespie, T. (2010). The Politics of "Platforms". *New Media & Society, 12,* 347–364. doi:10.1177/1461444809342738.

Gitelman, L. (2006). *Always Already New: Media, History, and the Data of Culture.* Cambridge, MA: MIT Press.

Grabher, G. (2004). Temporary Architectures of Learning: Knowledge Governance in Project Ecologies. *Organization Studies, 25,* 1491–1514.

Grant, R. M. (1996). Toward a Knowledge-Based Theory of the Firm. *Strategic Management Journal, 17*(Winter Special Issue), 109–122.

Greenberg, B., Sherry, J., Lachlan, K., Lucas, K., & Holmstrom, A. (2010). Orientations to Video Games Among Gender and Age Groups. *Simulation & Gaming, 41,* 238–259. doi:10.1177/1046878108319930.

Haas, P. (1992). Introduction: Epistemic Communities and International Policy Coordination. *International Organization, 46*(1), 1–35.

Hagiu, A. (2014). Strategic Decisions for Multisided Platforms. *MIT Sloan Management Review, 55,* 71–80.

Hall, S. (1980/1993). Encoding/Decoding. In S. During (Ed.), *The Cultural Studies Reader* (pp. 90–103). London: Routledge.

Hands, J. (2013). Introduction: Politics, Power and "Platformativity". *Culture Machine, 14.* Retrieved from http://www.culturemachine.net/index.php/cm/article/viewArticle/504

Hartley, J. (2008). *From the Consciousness Industry to Creative Industries: Consumer-Created Content, Social Network Markets and the Growth of Knowledge.* Retrieved November 10, 2008, from http://eprints.qut.edu.au/archive/00012642/

Helmond, A. (2015). The Platformization of the Web: Making Web Data Platform Ready. *Social Media + Society, 1*(11). doi:10.1177/2056305115603080.

Hienerth, C. (2004). *The Commercialization of User Innovations: The Development of the Kayak Rodeo Industry.* Retrieved February 14, 2008, from http://userinnovation.mit.edu/papers/Hienerth%20Commercializing%20UI.pdf

Hong, R., & Chen, V. H.-H. (2013). Becoming an Ideal Co-creator: Web Materiality and Intensive Laboring Practices in Game Modding. *New Media & Society, 1461444813480095.* doi:10.1177/1461444813480095.

Hou, J. (2011). Uses and Gratifications of Social Games: Blending Social Networking and Game Play. *First Monday, 16.*

Humphreys, S. (2008). Ruling the Virtual World: Governance in Massively Multiplayer Online Games. *European Journal of Communication, 11*(2), 149–172.

Huws, U. (2014). *Labor in the Global Digital Economy: The Cybertariat Comes of Age.* New York: Monthly Review Press.

Huysman, M., & de Wit, D. (2004). Practices of Managing Knowledge Sharing: Towards a Second Wave of Knowledge Management. *Knowledge and Process Management, 11*(2), 81–92.

Jenkins, H. (1992). *Textual Poachers: Television Fans & Participatory Culture.* London: Routledge.

Jenkins, H. (2006). *Convergence Culture: Where Old and New Media Collide.* New York: New York University Press.

Jeppesen, L. B. (2004). *Organizing Consumer Innovation: A Product Development Strategy That Is Based on Online Communities and Allows Some Firms to Benefit From a Distributed Process of Innovation by Consumers.* Unpublished Ph.D., Copenhagen Business School, Copenhagen.

Jeppesen, L. B., & Frederiksen, L. (2006). Why Do Users Contribute to Firm-Hosted User Communities?: The Case of Computer-Controlled Music Instruments. *Organization Science, 17*(1), 45–63.

Jeppesen, L. B., & Molin, M. J. (2003). Consumers as Co-developers: Learning and Innovation Outside the Firm. *Technology Analysis & Strategic Management, 15*(3), 363–384.

Johnson, R. (2013). Toward Greater Production Diversity: Examining Social Boundaries at a Video Game Studio. *Games and Culture, 8*(3), 136–160.

Kakihara, M., & Sørensen, C. (2002). Exploring Knowledge Emergence: From Chaos to Organizational Knowledge. *Journal for Global Information Technology Management, 5*(3), 48–66.

Karaganis, J. (Ed.). (2007). *Structures of Participation in Digital Culture.* New York: Social Science Research Council.

Kozinets, R. V. (1999). E-tribalized Marketing?: The Strategic Implications of Virtual Communities of Consumption. *European Management Journal, 17*(3), 252–264.

Kücklich, J. (2005). *Precarious Playbour: Modders and the Digital Games Industry.* Retrieved September 2, 2007, from http://journal.fibreculture.org/issue5/kuchlich.html

Kujala, S. (2003). User Involvement: A Review of the Benefits and Challenges. *Behaviour & Information Technology, 22*(1), 1–16.

Lakhani, K., & Wolf, R. (2003). *Why Hackers Do What They Do: Understanding Motivation Effort in Free/Open Source Software Projects*. Retrieved December 12, 2006, from http://freesoftware.mit.edu/papers/lakhaniwolf.pdf

Langlois, G., & Elmer, G. (2013). The Research Politics of Social Media Platforms. *Culture Machine, 14*, 1–17. Retrieved from http://www.culturemachine.net/index.php/cm/article/view-Article/505

Langlois, R., & Garzarelli, G. (2006). *Of Hackers and Hairdressers: Modularity and the Organizational Economics of Open-Source Collaboration*. Paper Presented at the Druid: Knowledge, Innovation and Competitiveness, Copenhagen.

Langlois, R., & Robertson, P. (1992). Networks and Innovation in a Modular System: Lessons from the Microcomputer and Stereo Component Industries. *Research Policy, 21*, 297–313.

Langlois, G., McKelvey, F., Elmer, G., & Werbin, K. (2009). Mapping Commercial Web 2.0 Worlds: Towards a New Critical Ontogenesis. *Fibreculture*, (14). Retrieved from http://fourteen.fibreculturejournal.org/fcj-095-mapping-commercial-web-2-0-worlds-towards-a-new-critical-ontogenesis/

Lau, G. (2005). *Developing Online Communities of Practice: A Case Study of the World of Warcraft*. Retrieved October 16, 2007, from http://polaris.gseis.ucla.edu/glau/courses/is209-paper.pdf

Lave, J., & Wenger, E. (1991). *Situated Learning: Legitimate Peripheral Participation*. Cambridge: Cambridge University Press.

Leadbeater, C., & Miller, P. (2004). *The Pro-Am Revolution: How Enthusiasts Are Changing Our Economy and Society*. London: Demos.

Lee, D. (2007). Creative London? Investigating New Modalities of Work in the Cultural Industries. In S. van der Graaf & Y. Washida (Eds.), *Information Communication Technologies and Emerging Business Strategies* (pp. 140–159). Hershey: Idea Group Publishing.

Lee, C. (2015). Participatory Practices in Organizations. *Sociology Compass, 9*(4), 272–288.

Lessig, L. (2004). *Free Culture*. New York: The Penguin Press.

Lettl, C., Herstatt, C., & Gemuenden, H. G. (2006). Users' Contributions to Radical Innovation: Evidence from Four Cases in the Field of Medical Equipment Technology. *R&D Management, 36*(3), 251–272.

Lévy, P. (1997). *Collective Intelligence: Mankind's Emerging World in Cyberspace*. Cambridge, MA: Perseus Books.

Li, C., & Bernoff, J. (2008). *Groundswell: Winning in a World Transformed by Social Technologies*. Boston: Harvard Business Press.

Lilien, G. L., Morrison, P. D., Searls, K., Sonnack, M., & von Hippel, E. (2002). Performance Assessment of the Lead User Idea Generation Process for New Product Development. *Management Science, 48*(8), 1042–1059.

Livingstone, S. (2003). *The Changing Nature of Audiences: From the Mass Audience to the Interactive Media User*. Retrieved August 9, 2008, from http://eprints.lse.ac.uk/archive/00000417

Livingstone, S. (2007). *Audiences and Interpretations*. Retrieved February 14, 2009, from http://eprints.lse.ac.uk/5645

Lueg, C. (2003). Knowledge Sharing in Online Communities and Its Relevance to Knowledge Management in the E-Business Era. *International Journal Electronic Business, 1*(2), 140–151.

Lundvall, B.-A. (1996). *The Social Dimension of the Learning Economy*. Retrieved February 17, 2007, from http://ssrn.com/abstract=66537

Lüthje, C. (2004). Characteristics of Innovating Users in a Consumer Goods Field: An Empirical Study of Sport-Related Product Consumers. *Technovation, 24*(9), 683–695.

Malone, T. (2004). *The Future of Work: How the New Order of Business Will Shape Your Organization, Your Management Style, and Your Life*. Cambridge, MA: Harvard Business School Press.

Mansell, R. (2012). *Imagining the Internet: Communication, Innovation, and Governance*. Oxford: Oxford University Press.

Mansell, R. (2016). *Unpacking Black Boxes: Understanding Digital Platform Innovation*. Drafte Information, Communication and Society. https://www.academia.edu/30175620/Unpacking_Black_Boxes_Understanding_Digital_Platform_Innovation

McRobbie, A. (2002). From Holloway to Hollywood: Happiness at Work in the New Cultural Economy? In P. du Gay & M. Pryke (Eds.), *Cultural Economy* (pp. 97–114). London: Sage.

Moody, K. A. (2014). *Modders: Changing the Game Through User-Generated Content and Online Communities*. Ph.D. (Doctor of Philosophy) Thesis, University of Iowa. http://ir.uiowa.edu/etd/4701

Morley, D. (1993). Active Audience Theory: Pendulums and Pitfalls. *Journal of Communication, 43*(4), 13–19.

Morrison, P. D., Roberts, J., & Midgley, D. (2004). The Nature of Lead Users and Measurement of Leading Edge Status. *Research Policy, 33*(2), 351–362.

Nieborg, D. B. (2005). *Am I Mod or Not? – An Analysis of First Person Shooter Modification Culture*. Paper Presented at the Creative Gamers Seminar – Exploring Participatory Culture in Gaming, University of Tampere.

Nieborg, D. B., & van der Graaf, S. (2008). The Mod Industries? The Industrial Logic of Non-market Game Production. *European Journal of Cultural Studies, 11*(2), 177–195.

Nonaka, I. (1991, November–December). The Knowledge Creating Company. *Harvard Business Review, 69*, 96–104.

O'Reilly, T. (2005). *What Is Web 2.0*. Retrieved October 4, 2008, from http://www.oreillynet.com/pub/a/oreilly/tim/news/2005/09/30/what-is-web-20.html

OECD. (2007). *Participative Web and User-Generated Content: Web 2.0, Wikis and Social Networking*. Paris: OECD Publishing.

Pearce, C. (2008). The Truth About Baby Boomer Gamers: A Study of Over-Forty Computer Game Players. *Games and Culture, 3*, 142–174. doi:10.1177/1555412005281418.

Piller, F. T., & Walcher, D. (2006). Toolkits for Idea Competitions: A Novel Method to Integrate Users in New Product Development. *R&D Management, 36*(3), 307–318.

Polanyi, M. (1969). *Knowing and Being: Essays by Michael Polanyi*. Chicago: The University of Chicago Press.

Postigo, H. (2007). Of Mods and Modders: Chasing Down the Value of Fan Based Digital Game Modifications. *Games and Culture, 2*(4), 300–313.

Postigo, H. (2008). Video Game Appropriation Through Modifications: Attitudes Concerning Intellectual Property among Fans and Modders. *Convergence: The International Journal of Research into New Media Technologies, 14*(1), 59–74.

Postigo, H. (2014). The Socio-technical Architecture of Digital Labor: Converting Play into YouTube Money. *New Media & Society*, 1–18. doi:10.1177/1461444814541527.

Potts, J., Cunningham, S., Hartley, J., & Ormerod, P. (2008). *Social Network Markets: A New Definition of the Creative Industries*. http://www.cultural-science.org/FeastPapers2008/JasonPotts1Bp.pdf

Powell, W. (1990). Neither Market nor Hierarchy: Network Forms of Organization. *Research in Organizational Behavior, 12*, 295–336.

Prahalad, C., & Krishnan, M. (2008). *The New Age of Innovation: Driving Co-created Value Through Global Networks*. New York: Mc Graw Hill.

Pratt, A. (2004). The Cultural Economy: A Call for Spatialized 'Production of Culture' Perspectives. *International Journal of Cultural Studies, 7*(1), 117–128.

Prax, P. (2016). *Co-creative Game Design as Participatory Alternative Media* (Uppsala Studies in Media and Communication 11). Uppsala: Acta Universitatis Upsaliensis. ISBN 978-91-554-9599-2.

Prügl, R., & Schreier, M. (2006). Learning From Leading-Edge Customers at the Sims: Opening Up the Innovation Process Using Toolkits. *R&D Management, 36*(3), 237–250.

Puschmann, C., & Burgess, J. (2013). *The Politics of Twitter Data.* HIIG Discussion Paper Series No. 2013-01. Retrieved from http://papers.ssrn.com/abstract=2206225

Rheingold, H. (1993). *The Virtual Community: Homesteading on the Electronic Frontier* (2001 MIT ed.). Cambridge, MA: MIT Press.

Rieder, B., & Sire, G. (2014). Conflicts of Interest and Incentives to Bias: A Microeconomic Critique of Google's Tangled Position on the Web. *New Media & Society, 16*, 195–211. doi:10.1177/1461444813481195.

Ritzer, G., & Jurgenson, N. (2010). Production, Consumption, Prosumption. *Journal of Consumer Culture, 10*(1), 13–36.

Rochet, J.-C., & Tirole, J. (2003). Platform Competition in Two-Sided Markets. *Journal of the European Economic Association, 1*, 990–1029. doi:10.1162/154247603322493212.

Rogers, E. (2003). *Diffusion of Innovations* (5th ed.). New York: Free Press.

Rogers, R. (2013). *Digital Methods.* Cambridge, MA: MIT Press.

Sapnar Ankerson, M. (2015, July–December). Social Media and the "Read-Only" Web: Reconfiguring Social Logics and Historical Boundaries. *Social Media + Society*, 1–12. doi:10.1177/2056305115621935.

Schäfer, M. (2008). *Bastard Culture! User Participation and the Extension of Cultural Industries.* Unpublished Ph.D., Utrecht University, Utrecht.

Shah, S. (2000). *Sources and Patterns of Innovation in a Consumer Products Field: Innovations in Sporting Equipment.* Retrieved August 4, 2008, from http://opensource.mit.edu/papers/shahsportspaper.pdf

Shah, S. K. (2006). Motivation, Governance, and the Viability of Hybrid Forms in Open Source Software Development. *Management Science, 52*(7), 1000–1014.

Shah, S., & Tripsas, M. (2004). *When Do User-Innovators Start Firms? Towards a Theory of User Entrepreneurship.* Retrieved August 4, 2008, from http://user-innovation.mit.edu/papers/Shah-Tripsas%20_2_%20%204-9-04.pdf

Shen, C., & Williams, D. (2011). Unpacking Time Online: Connecting Internet and Massively Multiplayer Online Game Use with Psychosocial Well-Being. *Communication Research, 38*, 123–149. doi:10.1177/0093650211037719.

Sotamaa, O. (2007). *On Modder Labour, Commodification of Play, and Mod Competitions.* Retrieved March 14, 2008, from http://www.uic.edu/htbin/cgiwrap/bin/ojs/index.php/fm/article/view/2006/1881

Steinkuehler, C. A. (2005). *Cognition & Learning in Massively Multiplayer Online Games: A Critical Approach.* Unpublished Ph.D., University of Wisconsin, Madison.

Striphas, T. (2015). Algorithmic Culture. *European Journal of Cultural Studies, 18*(4–5), 395–412.

Tamborini, R., Bowman, N., Eden, A., Grizzard, M., & Organ, A. (2010). Defining Media Enjoyment as the Satisfaction of Intrinsic Needs. *Journal of Communication, 60,* 758–777. doi:10.1111/j.1460-2466.2010.01513.x.

Teece, D. J. (1998). Capturing Value from Knowledge Assets: The New Economy, Markets for Know-How, and Intangible Assets. *California Management Review, 40*(3), 55–79.

Terranova, T. (2000). Free Labor: Producing Culture for the Digital Economy. *Social Text, 18*(2), 33–57.

Thomke, S., & von Hippel, E. (2002). Customers as Innovators: A New Way to Create Value. *Harvard Business Review, 80*(4), 74–81.

Ulrich, K. (1995). The Role of Product Architecture in the Manufacturing Firm. *Research Policy, 24,* 419–440.

UNESCO. (2007). *Kronberg Declaration on the Future of Knowledge Acquisition and Sharing.* Retrieved October 15, 2007, from http://www.unesco.de/kronberg_declaration.html?&L=0

van der Graaf, S. (2012a). Modonomics: Participation and Competition in Contention. *Journal of Gaming and Virtual Worlds, 4*(2), 119–135. Bristol: Intellect Ltd.

van der Graaf, S. (2012b). Get Organized at Work! A Look Inside the Game Design Process of Valve and Linden Lab. *Bulletin of Science, Technology & Society, 32*(6), 477–485.

van der Graaf, S., & Fisher, E. (2017). The Imperative of Code: Labour, Regulation and Legitimacy. In P. Meil & V. Kirov (Eds.), *The Policy Implications of Virtual Work* (pp. 109–135). New York: Palgrave.

van Dijck, J. (2009). Users Like You? Theorizing Agency in User-Generated Content. *Media Culture & Society, 31*(1), 41–58.

van Dijck, J. (2013). *The Culture of Connectivity: A Critical History of Social Media.* New York: Oxford University Press.

von Hippel, E. (1976). The Dominant Role of Users in the Scientific Instrument Innovation Process. *Research Policy, 5*(3), 212–239.

von Hippel, E. (1986). Lead Users: A Source of Novel Product Concepts. *Management Science, 32*(7), 791–805.

von Hippel, E. (1988). *The Sources of Innovation.* New York: Oxford University Press.

von Hippel, E. (1994). 'Sticky Information' and the Locus of Problem Solving: Implications for Innovation. *Management Science, 40*(4), 429–439.

von Hippel, E. (2001). Innovation by User Communities. *Trends in Communication: Communities of Practice, 8,* 37–44.

von Hippel, E. (2005). *Democratizing Innovation.* Cambridge, MA: MIT Press.

von Hippel, E., & Katz, R. (2002). Shifting Innovation to Users via Toolkits. *Management Science, 48*(7), 821–834.

von Krogh, G., Spaeth, S., & Lakhani, K. (2003). Community, Joining, and Specialization in Open Source Software Innovation: A Case Study. *Research Policy, 32*(7), 1217–1241.

Wadell, C., Ölundh Sandström, G., Björk, J., & Magnusson, M. (2013). Exploring the Incorporation of Users in an Innovating Business Unit. *International Journal of Technology Management, 61*(3/4), 293–308.

Washida, Y., Kinoshita, Y., & Awata, K. (2006). *Demand Side Innovation Hypothesis in the Complex Consumer Network.* Proceedings of Portland International Conference on Management of Engineering and Technology (PICMET'06), Portland, pp. 1749–1756.

Watts, D. J., & Dodds, P. S. (2007). *Influentials, Networks, and Public Opinion Formation.* Retrieved February 20, 2008, from http://cdg.columbia.edu/uploads/papers/watts2007_influentials.pdf

Wenger, E. (1998). *Communities of Practice: Learning, Meaning, and Identity.* Cambridge: Cambridge University Press.

Williams, D., Yee, N., & Caplan, S. (2008). Who Plays, How Much, and Why? Debunking the Stereotypical Gamer Profile. *Journal of Computer-Mediated Communication, 13,* 993–1018. doi:10.1111/j.1083-6101.2008.00428.x.

Williams, D., Consalvo, M., Caplan, S., & Yee, N. (2009). Looking for Gender (LFG): Gender Roles and Behaviors Among Online Gamers. *Journal of Communication, 59,* 700–725. doi:10.1111/j.1460-2466.2009.01453.x.

Williams, D., Kennedy, T., & Moore, R. (2010). Behind the Avatar: The Patterns, Practices and Functions of Role Playing in MMOs. *Games & Culture, 6,* 171–200. doi:10.1177/1555412 010364983.

Zittrain, J. (2008). *The Future of the Internet and How to Stop It.* New Haven: Yale University Press.

3

Game Changer

3.1   Design Capabilities

Linden Lab has created quite a game changer with its Second Life platform and service, providing various features that facilitate user participation to a far greater extent than previously. It warrants an investigation
into the users that donate time and labour to participate on the firm-
hosted platform. Insights into these questions about user participation
tend to have been approached in terms of cultural qualities (especially
with a tendency to overestimate creative capacities and contributions of
users and underestimate qualities of design and use), needs, and, often,
outside a commercial framework. This way downplays the dynamic of
user-technology interaction with the organizational socio-economic
structure. This chapter, therefore, begins the empirical journey towards
unravelling user participation on the Second Life platform. What follows
is the examination of participation patterns of the developer firm and
users in Second Life by relating disparities between user participation and
Second Life membership to the commencement of Linden Lab's brain-
child, highlighting the issue concerning the professionalization of user
participation in platform and product development. Several aspects of
user participation in the context of commercial and non-commercial

© The Author(s) 2018
S. van der Graaf, *ComMODify*, Dynamics of Virtual Work,
DOI 10.1007/978-3-319-61500-4_3

contributing developers on the Second Life platform are illuminated, guided by the *design capabilities* as a unit of analysis:

Design capabilities are idiosyncratic of particular participation patterns of users (or mod developers) and the developer firm that are, simultaneously, operating in the same designed space of Second Life. This links user participation and Second Life membership to the developer firm. Through interviews, web-based surveys and document data, the appeal of participating on the platform is explored and particular individual usage characteristics and communication behaviours of respondents are analysed. This informs the development of six Second Life user profiles. The investigation of design capabilities also draws attention to how the organization of the platform resonates with Linden Lab's organisational characteristics and internal culture. More precisely, both Linden Lab and Second life users are guided by processes of distributed design and distributed decision-making where people create, collaborate and, most importantly, are passionate about what they do. This highlights the issue of professionalization of mod development on the research agenda beyond common dichotomous play/labour debates.

3.2   The Making of Second Life

Second Life is the result of a series of course changes. In 1999, Linden Lab began working on a hardware feedback device ('haptics') that would enable users to fully immerse in virtual reality. In order to demonstrate this device (such as to potential investors), a virtual environment called 'Linden World', with task-based games, was built. The device was abandoned when the firm figured that Linden World had more potential, guiding the firm's choice to gear up towards a more lucrative opportunity of developing a software-based virtual environment. In retrospect, it can be said that Linden World was the first version of Second Life. The format of the 3D environment-to-be was set during a board meeting in 2001, when a number of people started creating on their own (such as snowmen). Those inputs hinted at what was to be the most compelling aspect of Second Life: people building and contributing own creations in real time. Rather than going for an objective-driven gaming experience common in other gaming and 3D software contexts, Linden Lab thus shifted its goals towards a user-created and community-driven platform. Jim, a software engineer at Linden Lab, points out the importance of user participation in Second Life.

> So from that point onwards, the whole of Linden Lab is very aware of the debt we owe to the people who are actually making stuff. I mean seriously, the Second Life platform is, you know, a fairly adequate piece of software that allows people to make all this cool stuff, and so there was an incredible awareness from very early on in what the users and residents of Second Life know, and what they can contribute.

This 'epiphany' encouraged around ten Linden Lab employees to work on transforming the Linden product into an avatar-based platform that allowed users to engage in building and eventually scripting activities. One year later, the alpha version of Second Life was up and running. In November 2002 Second Life entered a closed beta-testing phase and was opened up to users that were interested in assisting the firm with platform development. These 'early mod developers' (or, arguably lead users) lent a hand building and testing various aspects of the platform. In those days Second Life was basically a shared sandbox where, for example, it was possible to edit and move other people's avatars around. These user contributors were at the forefront of in-world content creation, collaboration and community building. They caused and/or witnessed Second Life's first encounters with, among others, combats and cheats.

On 23 June 2003 Second Life was released to the general public. It was Linden Lab's expectation that with an increase in content, Second Life would become more interesting for different kinds of users. In other words, it was the view of Linden Lab that the initial Second Life users were so-called 'early adopters' with a rather advanced skill level, but that, when time progressed and features were added, more average mod developers would join, followed by casual users that would participate in consumption rather than development practices. However, users did not exactly flock to Second Life. To draw in more users, users were granted intellectual property (IP) rights over their creations. Another change was to replace a subscription-based model with a variable pricing model whereby users paid in proportion to the size of land they used.[1] These changes gave Second Life its own sets of social norms, laws and markets (Ondrejka 2007).

In 2004, Linden Lab steered platform development towards in-world entrepreneurship through the Linden Dollar (L$). This resulted in an influx of users and an increase in monthly monetary exchanges between users. But it really was 2006 when Second Life made media headlines, in many cases marked by the entry of multiple 'first life' businesses. Adam, journalist for Reuters, describes how Reuters came to Second Life.

> This all got started when the Reuters CEO met the Linden CEO at a conference. [...] So a couple of months later they came to me and asked me first, if you have ever heard of this Second Life thing. And I said yah. But I never tried it. They said well, we want to open up a bureau there. Cover it like any other economy. And the idea seemed a bit outlandish at first but the more that I kind of looked into it, it really is a pretty good fit just because Second Life is an emerging economy just like a developing country in the real world. If it was just a video game, we wouldn't be there but because there is a real economy, because there is a real currency, because people own the concept that they create, it becomes possible for us to kind of cover this like we would a country in the real world.

By 2007, Second Life offered a home to roughly 11 million users that exchanged about US$ 8 million per month.[2] This steady increase in users and money may perhaps partially explain the number of firms such as Cisco and IBM that sought to develop an in-world presence for reasons such as marketing, training, experimentation and collaboration.[3] Another attractive incentive may have been Linden Lab's decision to open source the Second Life Client in that same year. Linden Lab reported that, although there were no libraries or extensive manuals and the like in place, the firm has received an increasing stream of user-developed contributions for integration in the Second Life platform (see Chap. 4). Overall, the development of Second Life is aptly captured by Linden Lab's 'Your World. Your Imagination'™.[4]

With the growth of the user base and the broadening of mod development opportunities, Second Life also produced a fair share of controversies. For example, despite Linden Lab's wish to refrain from platform governance, occasionally it had to interfere and make particular operational changes to its policies such as regarding sexual ageplay and wagering (which, in many cases, received user protests). Notwithstanding these concerns and other daily occurring incidents,[5] Second Life seems to have offered a spatialized real-time platform where all kinds of users from all over the world can interact with others, engage in creative activities (of a commercial and non-commercial nature), and can belong to various communities at once. Now let's take a closer look at what draws people to the platform.

3.3   X-Factor

As discussed in the previous chapter, several studies have produced insights into user motivations underlying their participation in innovation, in general, and mod development, in particular. Motivations include career advancement, reputation, social interactions, escapism, learning, achievement, power, creativity and play (Behr 2007; Consalvo 2007; Schultheiss 2007; Sotamaa 2004; van der Graaf 2012). What were the motivations of Second Life users in its heyday?

For this study, the appeal of Second Life was measured in terms of social, topical and technical aspects. The survey statements explored relationships ('I can enjoy social interactions with others' and 'I can help others with building, scripting and texturing'), escapism ('I can pretend to be someone else'), creativity ('I like to build, script and/or texture' and 'I can modify Second Life Open Source'), peer recognition ('I can build a reputation') and innovation potential ('It is innovative', 'I like that we can retain intellectual property rights' and 'I can make money').[6] The findings from 434 Second Life users showed that its appeal lay particularly in the enjoyment of social interactions, innovation and building, script and/or texture practices. Also, retention of intellectual property rights, earning an income, reputation building, helping others with development practices and pretending to be someone else are important; and, for a smaller group, being able to modify Second Life open source was an important draw.

These results appear to be consistent with other studies (Banks 2013; Nood and Attema 2007; Ortiz de Gortari 2007). The mean outcomes show that Second Life attracts users that are interested in the platform's offerings of sociability and, in particular, in-world creativity. For instance, Strife, a user interviewed for this study, sums up his reasons for participation:

Interests: socializing, scripting, building.

Second Life might also mean an escape from real-life physical disabilities, social, financial and other constraints. Adeel, who suffers from cerebral palsy and is on disability benefits, describes why he participates in Second Life:

I am very lonely in R[eal] L[ife]. When I go out to social events, or help like after the hurricane Katrina I meet people and they have their own worlds and I am like a meteor floating in space. After helping, everyone went on their way and left me behind. And [I] went to Active Worlds. People were so 'indifferent' and cold. I find SL to be more friendly. This is my main Gorean set. I would like to learn how to make money here.

Mike, a teen user, described his interest in Second Life as driven by creative endeavours, as he is interested in pixel design. The first time he heard about Second Life, however, he did not sign up because it was then for adults only.

So all of a sudden two years later, I am looking for buildings because I like to draw things I see in pixel. And all of a sudden I saw this 3D picture of a building that a teen made and I was like I want to do that. So then got myself an account. And the first day I signed on, I was like there is other people walking around. I was like wow.

For Garrett, another interviewee, Second Life offered the opportunity to explore alternative means to conduct his business as an interaction and interface designer. Because he had been in software development for over a decade he had developed a pragmatic (and, a somewhat cynical) approach to new technologies. Yet, his attention was drawn to the complexity of the interface and user experience of Second Life, which could support (showcasing) his skills and improve his business.

> The need to get the word out and at the same time an increasingly acceptance by clients to receive their work digitally and not ever physically meet, as well the growth and pervasiveness of broadband and my desire to work in an international marketplace led me to consider another method of communication.

The findings also show that, in accordance with the prospect of content creation, IP ownership is deemed a relatively appealing feature for user involvement. Scores, however, concerning escapism and advanced creativity (that is, open source) lean towards neutrality, which confirms earlier findings. The advanced creativity result may be partially explained by the timing of this survey, which was conducted roughly five months after Linden Lab's announcement of open sourcing the client software and a community had not yet established. Another reason may be related to the advanced skills and the know-how needed to mod the client code, capabilities that majority users do not tend to have (von Hippel 2005; Behr 2007).

The survey also asked respondents to rank six items concerning the appeal of Second Life in order of importance. Again, social interactions followed by user creativity were considered the most important aspects for participation. Making money and purchasing behaviour ranked after the relative importance of visual appearance of one's avatar and/or home and attending in-world activities. In sum, users are attracted for mostly social and creative motivations. Let's now have a closer look at the users that participate in Second Life.

3.4   The Many Lives of Second Life

Second Life is mostly praised for its generative features that inform the dynamic relationship between user participation as input and user innovation as output. This generative capacity is a quality that thrives on unexpected and unfiltered modifications and contributions made by all kinds of users (Zittrain 2008). In order to learn more about those contributing users several studies were consulted that have produced various taxonomies, such as those based on player styles, individual traits and friendship, and gamers' relations to the rules of the game.[7] Yet, there does not seem to be one typology of 'the' user-as-participant nor what her/his particular participation patterns are in the context of the firm underpinning online product development. Moreover, a systematic empirically grounded investigation of ways users participate on firm-hosted platforms, what they may contribute, how and with what frequency they may interact with others cannot be detected easily.

For these reasons, this book's empirical investigation of Second Life users results in a topology of memberships, profiled against following *participation qualities*: participation patterns, communication behaviour and several general user characteristics (cf. de Valck 2005; Wiertz and Ruyter 2007). Based on survey data, four classification variables were developed: (1) duration of in-world visits, (2) design capabilities (building, texturing, scripting, open sourcing), (3) information retrieval, and (4) supply. They served as input for the cluster analysis. More specifically: in-world visits provided insight into average duration of weekly Second Life visits; building, texturing, scripting, open sourcing are considered main formats of contribution to mod development practices, underpinning the development of the Second Life platform; information retrieval, that is, reading the blog, forums, scripters/developers mailing list, open source/Linden scripting language portal, in-world group message; and information supply, that is, post blog script, forums, scripters/developers mailing list, open source/Linden scripting language portal, in-world group messages. These all yield insight into participation in social interactions.

First, a hierarchical clustering method was employed to give an indication of the number of clusters to be utilized in the non-hierarchical clustering method.[8] The six-cluster solution was preferred, providing a wider and richer systematic understanding of various elements underpinning participation qualities in the context of the firm than previous studies have accounted for. Each cluster represents a particular Second Life user membership according to her/his participation patterns and communication behaviour on the Second Life platform.

Twink The first cluster groups 15% of the respondents. Each week, these users spend 9–15 hours in Second Life. They have used tools to build, texture, and, particularly, script, and they have an interest in modding the Second Life Viewer. Furthermore, the respondents are rather passively involved in platform communications by mainly retrieving information that is provided on the blog, forums, mailing lists, wiki portal and in-world. The blog, Linden Scripting Language (LSL) portal, and in-world group messages are read on a weekly basis, whereas the other communication means are less frequently read (only a few times per month). This group hardly ever supplies information to the Second Life community. If they do participate in information supply, it tends to be on the blog (via comments), forums, scripters mailing list and in-world group messages.

Newb The second cluster contains the largest group of respondents (26%). They also spend weekly 9–15 hours in Second Life and are potentially interested in engaging in building activities. There is no pro/con attitude towards the other tools for creative endeavours. The respondents' communication behaviours indicate that they are not actively involved in the community. The forums and in-world messages are only read a few times per month and contributions are seldom made to in-world group chats.

Pro The third cluster accounts for 17% of the respondents. These Second Life users tend to be more actively involved than users of the first two clusters. They spend between 25 and 40 hours per week in-world, where they repeatedly engage in building practices. Particularly, they take part in scripting activities. The respondents are heavy users of the in-world messaging system. On a daily basis messages are read and a few times per week messages are supplied. The forums, however, are used only on a monthly basis where a similar amount of information is retrieved and supplied. They are not active readers of the blog, but do comment once or twice a month. The LSL portal is read a few times per month, whereas the mailing lists and the open-source portal hardly ever get read. Contributions to these channels are not made.

Power Rezzer This is the smallest cluster containing 9% of the respondents. These users also spend 25–40 hours per week in-world. Building and texturing are their core activities. They have engaged in scripting and would be interested in contributing to open sourcing Second Life. From their communication behaviour, it can be gathered that this group of users is an active bunch that is highly vested in Second Life. The respondents are 'power users' in their behaviour of both retrieving and supplying information. In-world messages are read on a daily basis. The forums, scripters and developers mailing lists and LSL portal are read a few times a week, while the blog and open-source portal are read once or twice per month. Power Rezzers also supply information. A few times per month they contribute to the blog, forums, mailing lists and LSL portal.

Facilitator The fifth cluster is the second smallest group consisting of 11% of the respondents. Facilitators spend each week 16–24 hours in-world. Similar to the first cluster, these Second Life users have engaged in building, texturing and scripting activities yet do not seem to have a particular dis/interest in open source. Their communication patterns are quite different however. The respondents show a strong interest in the communal aspects of the Second Life community by reading the blog, forums and in-world messages on a daily basis. To a lesser extent, information is read on the LSL portal, scripter's mailing list and open-source portal. Information is also supplied to those channels, however, on a less frequent basis; once or twice a week contributions are made to the forums and in-world messages, and a few times each month, comments are made to the blog.

Experience Broker The final cluster constitutes 22% of the respondents. Each week users spend 16–24 hours in Second Life. Building is their main activity, while some experience with texturing is reported. No particular dis/interest can be detected in scripting, yet no ambition seems to exist for these users to contribute to open-source activities. Users of this cluster are fairly engaged in reading (mostly) in-world group messages, the blog and forums. Information is also supplied but less frequently than it is retrieved. Monthly contributions are made to in-world messages and the forums, while the respondents rarely comment on the blog.

A further examination of the cluster solutions on several additional variables was conducted as a means to enhance user membership profiles.

The findings indicated that there is a significant association between selected gender among the six user types. In the first five clusters men outnumber women, however, there are more women among experience brokers. This may indicate that women prefer a type of communication behaviour that seems especially directed towards the community, namely the blog, forums and in-world messaging. The smallest difference (in %) according to gender is for the newb cluster. Assuming joining Second Life is not sex-biased, this finding may indicate that men and women have similar initial exploratory engagements (before settling on particular practices). In addition, the variables year of registration, membership type, land ownership, age, income, monthly expenditures, monthly sales and monthly account balance were used for further profiling the six membership types.[9]

The results of year of registration indicate that of all the clusters Newbs have joined Second Life most recently. These newbs also tend to have an 'additional basic' account, while the respondents of the other clusters appear to have a type of premium account. The mean values of land ownership indicate that the respondents, (except cluster two that consists of former land owners) tend to rent land. The monthly average expenditure seems to be linked to those membership types where users spend the most time in Second Life, that is, Pros, Power Rezzers, Facilitators and Experience Brokers. Furthermore, the account balance scores seem to be consistent with the developed profiles in that Newbs have the lowest account balance, while the Power Rezzers have the highest, which seems to support their full-on participation in mod development practices. However, Facilitators not Power Rezzers have the highest mean value for approximate monthly sales. A strong overall involvement in mod development practices (and, in the case of Power Rezzers, an interest in open source) therefore, does not necessarily seem to equate to, or translate into commercial activity.

This draws attention to the organization of interdependent relationships developing between multiple spheres of economic activity that underpin the firm-hosted 3D platform. The aim of the following section, therefore, is to connect the organization of the developer firm to mod development. It investigates the complexities of crossover labour processes on the firm-hosted platform indicative of the professionalization and commercialization of user participation in Second Life.

3.5   The Developer Firm as Employer

So, what does Linden Lab want? To answer this strategic question, let us take a look Linden Lab's mission statement at the time it developed Second Life. Referred to as 'Tao of Linden', it describes principles underlying the attitude and approach towards being employed, a Linden, at the firm.[10] It stresses, among other things, the freedom to choose what to work on, transparency and openness, no hidden agendas and office politics, taking pleasure in work, and, to do all that with 'style'.[11] Running and nurturing Linden Lab in this way goes back to the firm's early days when it was still a small start-up.

In those days, Linden Lab consisted of a handful of developers and an office manager. Some had already worked at other companies and, based on those encounters with corporate culture, they sought to avoid particular negative experiences. One advantage of being a small company was the (relatively) flat hierarchy, allowing input and decision-making from all Lindens. Internally, discussions could be held about what kind of attributes of the 'Linden culture to be' would be desirable. At the same time, they had to take into account whether these 'work ways' could be sustained over time in a growing company. Linden Lab came up with four goals that were to underpin Linden Lab's culture: (1) to maintain a flat hierarchy; (2) to make Linden Lab a fun place to work; (3) to refrain from ideas of ownership of (bits of) code; and (4) to have no meetings, or as few meetings as possible.

In fact, since those early days, Linden Lab has prided itself on its effort to give all employees the chance to opt-in by their choice to commit to and execute outstanding job tasks. The practice of opting-in is based on volitional commitment. Linden Lab has developed a near 100% commitment to having employees choose what to work on (cf. Griffin 2017). This devotion towards employee participation in employment arrangements suggests an entrepreneurial outlook concerning work. In other words, having Lindens set their own strategic direction, as envisaged by founder and former CEO Philip Rosedale, reveals a strategy whereby everyone employed at Linden Lab should think and behave like an entrepreneur. This practice of entrusting Lindens to opt-in comes with the expectation that they choose work wisely and execute it. In other words, Lindens are held responsible for carefully selecting work from outstanding job tasks according to their own skill set and preferences for particular tasks, and they are held accountable for successfully accomplishing a chosen task. With this practice of distributed entrepreneurship, it is not a surprise that Linden Lab appeared on the 2007 and 2008 lists as one of the most democratic workplaces in the world.[12]

With over 200 employees, Linden Lab operates a distributed office structure, where people can work remotely, and may or may not frequent the headquarters in San Francisco.[13] The largest group of 'remote Lindens' is made up of 'Liaisons', official client-facing Lindens by providing in-world help to Second Life users. One of the interviewees, Torley, who made it from early Second Life user to community management to product manager, has never set foot in Linden Lab's offices:

> I've never met them in person ... yet! I sure feel part of Linden Lab though, because it is a philosophy unto its own. My perspectives on existence and such have always been pretty lateral, so I'm very happy to be working at such a seemingly unorthodox company.

A practice that strengthens bonds between scattered Lindens like Torley, and enforces Linden Lab's commitment to openness and transparency among Lindens, is what is called 'Achievements and Objectives' (As & Os). This is a weekly email sent out by Lindens to the rest of the company, containing what they are working on and what their goals are by reporting As & Os for that particular week. It is not likely that the majority of Lindens sift through all these weekly emails, but the interviewees consistently reported reading the ones sent out by colleagues that work on tasks that are of direct interest or concern.

Another mechanism for Linden Lab to organize work was the third party tool JIRA.[14] It is used to communicate, manage and organize asynchronous tasks, projects and documents underlying product development. Internally, JIRA is mainly employed in support of active development practices, while externally (or, client-facing), it is predominantly used as a means to gather feedback from Second Life users. In other words, JIRA provides an overview of all outstanding and performed tasks, bugs and other issues, guiding Lindens on a daily basis to enter and pick tasks underlying Linden Lab's internal operations.[15]

Second Life itself is also regarded as a tool that effectively deals with geographical and organizational constraints, allowing (dispersed) Lindens to collaborate and communicate. More specifically, Linden Lab employs its own product and service platform to build and maintain its culture among the various (and dispersed) teams. This central role of within-firm deployment of Second Life, however, may not be obvious to a new Linden. It is known that a new hire might mistakenly assume sharing the same office equals physical proximity rather than logging onto Second Life (see Chap. 5). The platform provides open and certain closed areas for Lindens, which are frequently used for, among other things, meetings, presentations and job interviews. Brett, a web content editor at Linden Lab, was hired after his in-world interview:

> I actually literally went out and bought like an avatar suit. You know, because you want to make a good impression and I didn't know if that was necessary or not but I figured, you know, I'll lean towards the conservative just to be on the safe side. And so I did that and I had the actual in-world interview. This was before voice. [...] So it was all text chat. The in-world experience interview was with two people that I now work with pretty much on a daily basis.

So Linden Lab not only develops Second Life but also inhabits its product or design space for firm-related tasks. In this way, Lindens often (albeit, at times, in different vicinities) rub shoulders with mod developers. The previous section laid down profiles of Second Life users, but what kind of people work at Linden Lab? Smart, creative, energetic and passionate (SCEP) people are the qualities that Linden Lab looks for when hiring people.

> The reality right now is that for the most part it is pretty decentralized. I mean the idea is that you as a contributor, any individual worker there, bring whatever talents or skill sets that they hired you for to the table and you seek out. You know it's very transparent. (Brett)

> Almost everything here is your own initiative, the timid need not apply lol. (Blue)

It is not unheard of that applicants are interviewed eight to ten times. Moreover, similar to other developer firms, engineers have to undergo a 'programming test' focusing on algorithmically complex problems as part of the hiring process (cf. van der Graaf and Cobarr 2008). The point of these tests is not so much to make applicants come up with right solutions, but rather to find people that regard such complexities as 'irresistible' and are capable of justifying choices made and programming languages chosen. Job seekers applying for various permanent and temporary positions may stem from the Second Life community and elsewhere. For example, one of the Second Life community interviewees was commissioned by Linden Lab to work on the setup of Orientation Island.

> It's a job on the side, very much or rather a hobby that pays. I can't downgrade the research or teaching work I do because I'm getting $ from Second Life. That's all based on time spent, it's not something that's possible to really leave off or do part-time. I know quite a few of the Linden Lab people. I have been to their Second Life Views thing etc. and I think the Orientation Island team just don't have the manpower, so I think Torley suggested me to them. (Seifert)

Despite many applications, Linden Lab finds it hard to attract people with the right combination of qualifications; exceptional skills and/or a really good resume as well as fitting the Linden profile. Not only does Linden Lab compete with other digital firms like Google, but also with the Second Life community at large. There are thousands of businesses that have set up shop in Second Life, and in various capacities, tend to depend on skills possessed by other users. This has resulted in manifold Second Life-related jobs, varying from contracting to full-time positions that may, by some users, be considered more attractive or suitable than working for Linden Lab.

3.6 The Developer Community as Employer

The six membership types illustrate how Second Life offers a plethora of creative opportunities where users with different levels of skills and know-how can participate. Regardless of incentive and skill to participate in mod development, users (as individuals and as collectives) can make their mods and/or skills available (for free or a fee) for others to copy, rework or simply use. Such practices highlight the opportunities for entrepreneurship created and ways employment can be organized among mod developers on the firm-hosted platform. Showing what you can do is an important requisite in this context. For many, Second Life offers a place for users to rez,[16] or show each other one's objects and development. This act of showcasing can be understood as a communicative (and aesthetic) experience and is pivotal for in-world interactions. Showing work to others means sharing an understanding of the roads that were travelled to arrive at the current path and which may lead to work. Mike (Teen Grid) recalled a situation where he was on some land watching newcomers at work. Soon he learned that they were trying out for 'Skoolaborate', which was an Australian initiative that used Second Life as a means to engage students in collaborative learning experiences. Mike sent in his buildings and got the job.

> He almost thought I was an adult. He didn't understand. Yah. Pretty nice. [...] I am getting paid like two grand. [...] They really want me to help them out, get started off in Second Life because I am like the little guru kid. They kind of want to help me out getting a business started.

An early example of a Second Life-based company was The Electric Sheep Company (TESC, 2006–2012). Its founder, Sibley had an interest in building a communication platform where social interactions could blend with ecommerce. Second Life seemed a good match. He hired someone in 2005 to set up the company and in 2006 committed himself full-time. Within one year, TESC had twenty-five employees who were mainly preoccupied with offering in-world professional services for clients such as advertising and public relations agencies. The company's relationship with Linden Lab was highly regarded, not only in terms of what it launched in Second Life from which Linden Lab could benefit, but also in terms of pushing the boundaries of the platform itself.

> We talk to [Linden Lab] several times a week. [...] How much work would it be to do this? When is this feature coming out? And then just generally

being in touch with what is going on. We try to steer away from this but there occasionally are projects where we go and are jointly with the client in some cases, specifically asking Linden Lab to roll out a particular feature a little bit sooner so we can use it if it is really critical for a particular project. [...] If it is a feature that is not at all on their road map, then they in theory might do it for pay but in practice they won't because they are totally busy. But usually it is something they wanted to do. It is a matter of just moving it up to be done sooner. (Sibley)

Other interviewees reported not to have benefited from such a form of 'favouritism'. An explanation may be related to the size of the project (in other words, money), or, more likely, to the tremendous growth the platform experienced alongside the recognition of professional standards of running a business like Linden Lab. In particular, when technical aspects fail and Linden Lab does not prioritize an issue, the dependency of mod developers on the developer firm becomes apparent. For example, land-owner Garrett explained that his client-facing and paid-for project 'Swissopolis' was extremely delayed because he found no immediate response and/or action by Linden Lab regarding several technical issues such as developing the largest terra form ever attempted in-world, namely the Matterhorn at Second Life scale. It was built as part of a highly trafficked set of islands with embedded premium first-life brands rather than concentrating on a single brand. It would have been a first if the project had received a more adequate response from the developer firm, which would have prevented rising costs (and delay in income) that directly impacted the labour process, as there was no longer sufficient money to hire skilled builders and scripters for an extensive period of time to allow a quick turn-around in delivering the project. In the meantime, Linden Lab launched Bay City, which was built with the same strategy in mind, and became a strong competitor.

Employers that wish to attract hires for various paid and unpaid jobs, varying from employment arrangements of a more temporary nature to full-time positions, also tend to fish in the user pond. In so doing, they compete with Linden Lab and many small and large-sized, first and Second Life-based entrepreneurs in search for talented mod developers.

Generally, job openings and service offerings tend to be announced in a dedicated section on the Second Life forum, in paid-for advertisements in-world, or by referral such as via in-world groups and friends. Tedd, an open-source developer from Norway, joined Second Life to check out its technology and dabble in some business opportunities. He was not interested, however, in learning yet another programming language, but in the idea of building a Second Life server and via an email list came across a group of like-minded individuals.

> I really started to feel the need of programming again because two weeks without programming must be a record or something [...] So I joined them basically just on the IRC channel asking what they needed help with. [...] And they said that they needed scripting. I had some experience with writing some script engines before so I started on that. [...] And I think within a week or something then they had given me membership in the core group or something because the amount of code that I was delivering was too much to put into the project, so that is the acceptance limit or threshold to accept new members [...].

This open-source initiative became known as OpenSimulator Project (or, 'OpenSim'), operating on the Second Life server-side with the aim of making Second Life interoperable with other 3D environments.[17] OpenSim serves as an entity where people can donate, for example, licensing rights to developers for using tools, making it commercially friendly and may facilitate entrepreneurship (see Chaps. 4 and 5).

Similar to Linden Lab's objectives concerning potential hires, mod employers seek to select the right person for the job based on skills and experience as well as on personality. When employers deal with remote workers they have never met and who, in many cases, are only known by their Second Life name, personality is an important attribute. Garrett explains:

> What I have come the conclusion of, with all these people, the same conclusion they all come to is that what we're really looking for now is the temperament, the personality. That we can build on. Because if you don't got that, it doesn't matter if you have the skills. You can't be trusted, or you're not disciplined, you're not responsible.

Mod developers use Second Life as their object of work and/or the environment they work in, and as their preferred means of communication with their peers; especially, chat, instant message and more recently, voice assist them in the organization of work.[18] Second Life furthermore supports infrastructure for commercial endeavours, allowing users to transfer money via an internal micro payment system. The client-side of previously mentioned JIRA is used by the mod developer community to report bugs and, to a lesser extent, request features. While it notifies Linden Lab of submitted issues, JIRA also helps the wider community in communicating other contributors' interests and issues that may inform mod developers to support entered issues by casting their vote. The type of call and eloquence of discussions does not only make a stronger case to Linden Lab, indicating what actions to prioritize. It may also lead to opportunities for mod developers to collaborate.

Looking then at the work arrangements at Linden Lab and, now, within the mod development domain, Linden Lab's internal organization can be said to reflect the firm's dedication to user participation in platform development. Both Lindens and Second Life users operate 'entrepreneur-like', work the same space, use, in many cases, similar tools, and in their activities are part of a collaborative effort to make the firm-hosted 3D platform a better and more enticing place that is adjustable to each person's liking.

3.7   Conclusion: Patterns of User Participation

This chapter has examined the creative capacities of users and their contributions to platform development in the commercial setting of the developer firm Linden Lab. The analysis was designed to enhance our understanding of user participation on a firm-hosted platform. By drawing out design capabilities as a unit of empirical scrutiny, Second Life membership was related to within-firm organization of Linden Lab. The underlying aim for doing this was to demonstrate particular qualities of user participation.

Linden Lab was assessed as a developer firm that has embraced and fully integrated user participation in its overarching strategy, highlighting a 'break' with a more traditional perspective on vertical organization of within-firm development activities. The analysis also showed that Linden Lab's initial interest was a technological orientation, which changed direction over time. By 2002 Linden Lab had thought out the alpha version of the user-centred 3D environment Second Life, thereby already showing early signs of user creation, community building and collaboration. Crucial in the development process and in popularizing Second Life was Linden Lab's abandonment of the practice to own the IP of user-generated content and to replace a subscription-based model with a variable-pricing model. In a little under ten years, Linden Lab saw itself, and its product, grow from a small- to a medium-sized software service platform that, on a daily basis, handles roughly half a million users.

By examining work arrangements at Linden Lab and within the mod development domain, this study sought to move beyond the (narrow) focus on culture of mod development per se associated with user participation in the context of firm. The findings begin to unravel the complexity of (emerging) norms and values of user participation on the firm-hosted platform, catering to the developer firm and mod developers. Both firm and developers tend to look for new talent in-world and deem someone's skills important but personality even more so, as is an entrepreneurial (and accountable) attitude and approach to work. Both firm and developers are developers and users of tools and technologies, and seem to benefit from the platform and community for commercial and non-commercial reasons.

So, whereas some evidence does highlight a likelihood that users may develop an *entrepreneurial* approach towards their own participation in Second Life underpinning a rapidly growing in-world economy, the findings indicated that most users are less motivated by monetary rewards, relative to other drivers, to join or participate in Second Life. In accordance with earlier research findings, the analysis showed that the main reasons attracting users to Second Life were three-fold: social interactions, creativity and the innovation potential.

In order to yield insight into the prevalence of users drawn to this 3D platform, and particular capabilities that characterize these users, a two-step cluster analysis was conducted. The analysis resulted in six membership profiles that were based on individual participation patterns, communication behaviour and several additional variables, that is, year of registration, membership type, land ownership, age, income, monthly expenditures, monthly sales and monthly account balance. They are presented in Fig. 3.1. The development of six user profiles suggests that nuances exist. Although this outcome should not be taken normatively, it does provide a systematic, broader and richer understanding of the various qualities that underpin participation in the context of product development practices (than, for example, a more dichotomous approach discerning between participating and non-participating users).

The findings reveal a strong interdependence between the developer firm and mod developers. As a result, the (distributed) organizational design and the practice of user participation are viewed as two complementary sources underlying platform development. In other words, a dynamic tension between emergent and designed properties among the

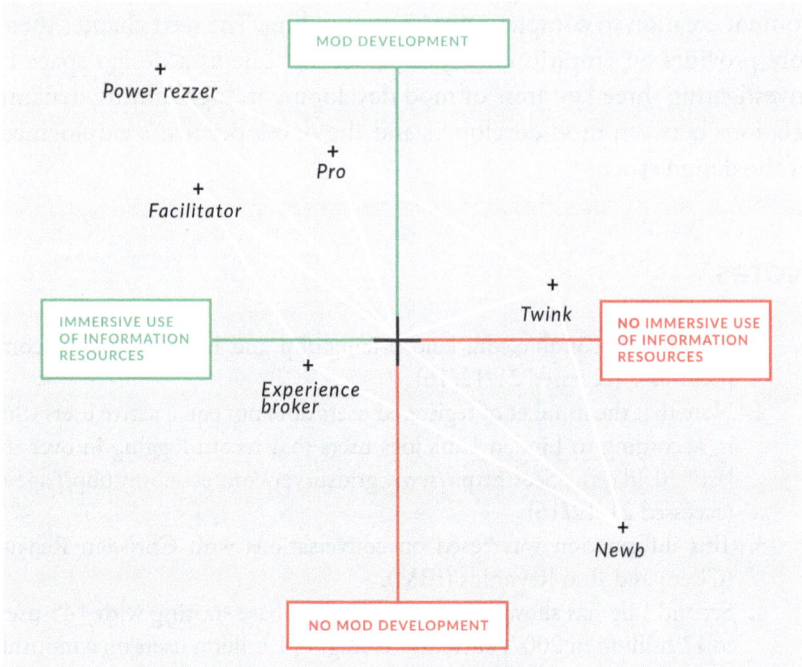

Fig. 3.1   User participation profiles of Second Life users

firm and developers is emphasized. This dynamic between top-down and bottom-up expressions of platform development, between institutional design and emergent practices, makes the issue of professionalism of user participation explicit. In fact, what is at stake is not so much the investigation of user participation in mod development practices in terms of play/labour, but rather a type of outsourcing 2.0 where the developer firm relies on its user base for product or platform development. Furthermore, this may, at the same time, indicate a participation tipping point, highlighting the prospect that users themselves can become entrepreneurs, while drawing attention to the firm (that still provides and/or hosts the platform) but becomes a 'reversed participant' or client of mod developments.

Within this setting, it is pivotal to understand what the firm-provided design space is in terms of the parameters and conditions that underlie the organizational and technical elements of the platform through which the firm develops and organizes user participation, varying from basic content creation to complex open-source coding. The next chapter therefore provides an empirical analysis of Second Life as a design space by investigating three key areas of mod development, highlighting dynamic relations between mod developers and the developer firm's employment of the design space.

Notes

1. See http://secondlife.com/land/pricing.php and http://secondlife.com/premium/ (accessed 21/12/16).
2. Note that the number of registered users does not equal active users (that is, according to Linden Lab's logs users that record logging in over the last 30 days). See http://www.gridsurvey.com/economy.php?page=1 (accessed 21/12/16).
3. This information was based on conversations with Christian Renaud (Cisco) and Roo Reynolds (IBM).
4. Second Life has shown an expanding user base starting with 145 users to 11 million in 2007, currently averaging 1 million users on a monthly basis. The number of Linden Lab employees ('Lindens') has grown

from 5 in 2000, to 220 in 2007 and has about 245 in 2016. Also, note that since 2013 Linden Lab has operated Blocksworld (a 'build and play' system for the iPad targeted at kids and adults) and, in early 2017, it is set to launch Sansar, a new platform to create social virtual reality experiences, suggesting Second Life has been handled by fewer Lindens over the past five years or so. See https://www.lindenlab.com/about (19/12/16).

5. See http://www.gridsurvey.com/blotter.php for Linden Lab's daily incident report including types of violations and actions undertaken by Linden Lab.

6. The findings also indicates that more men than women participated in *Second Life* (N = 434), 58.8% vs. 35.9%). The mean age of the respondents was 34.49 with a median age of 34 and a range from 13 to 68. By far the largest groups of respondents resided in North America (58%) and Europe (32%). Nearly half of the respondents were said to work full-time and about one-third of the respondents earned an annual income less than US$ 30,000. See http://etheses.lse.ac.uk/100/ for all statistical information used in this book (in particular, Chap. 5).

7. See Chap. 2. Also, older orientations were consulted such as a 'lurker/poster' dichotomy (or, passive/active participation) (Rheingold 1993), location of consumption practice (Cova and Cova 2002; Li and Bernoff 2008), and social and topical involvement (Crowston and Howison 2005; Kozinets 1999).

8. The latter method is considered to be less myopic and better able to withstand irrelevant variables, outliers and the distance measure deployed than hierarchical clustering methods (Field 2005). The hierarchical cluster analysis used Ward's Method, using the squared Euclidian distance measure. Based on the outcome of the hierarchical cluster analysis and in accordance with previous research, four to eight cluster solutions and order solutions were executed during the non-hierarchical K-Means clustering (Valck 2005). See http://etheses.lse.ac.uk/100/ for all statistical information used in this book (in particular, the Annex).

9. Levene's test for *monthly sales/income* was < .05. Only Welch F for *sales* was significant and reported. The results of the one-way between-groups ANOVA with post-hoc tests reported significant effects of the variables on the six membership clusters and making the six profiles rounder and deeper. Respectively, year of registration (F $(5, 428)$ = 7.361, p < .001, ω = 0.24); membership (F $(5, 428)$ = 9.864, p < .001, ω = 0.96); land

ownership (F (5, 428) = 13.947, $p < .001$, ω = 0.36); age (F (5, 423) = 3.098, $p \leq .001$, ω = 0.14); approximate expenditure per month (L\$) (F (5, 387) = 11.431, $p < .001$, ω = 0.35); approximate account balance per month (L\$) (F (5, 360) = 10.051, $p < .001$, ω = 0.33); and, approximate sales per month. (L\$) (Welch F (5, 139) = 23.045, $p < .001$, ω = 0.4). Note: for *sales* the homogeneity of variance assumption was broken, therefore the Welch F was used and year of registration and age have a small effect. Land ownership, expenditure, account balance and sales have a medium effect. Membership has a large effect (Field 2005).

10. See https://community.secondlife.com/t5/Features/The-Tao-of-Linden/ba-p/521028/ (accessed 21/12/16).
11. Ibid.
12. See http://www.worldblu.com/awardee-profiles/2008.php (accessed 21/12/16).
13. Linden Lab also has offices in Boston, Seattle, Davis and Charlottesville. In 2010 they closed some offices including one in the UK and The Netherlands.
14. See https://jira.secondlife.com/secure/Dashboard.jspa (accessed 21/12/16).
15. Lindens cast their vote on unresolved issues they deem worthwhile, which results in a ranking system that guides the (de)prioritization of particular issues.
16. Rezzing is akin to a handshake in the real world.
17. See http://opensimulator.org/wiki/Main_Page/ (accessed 21/12/16).
18. Interviewees also reported using external communication means such as Skype for video and voice conferencing, and IRC seems to be the main channel for open source developers.

References

Banks, J. (2013). *Co-creating Videogames*. New York: Bloomsbury.
Behr, K.-M. (2007). *The Development of Computer Game Modifications: Creators of Games Content Explored*. Paper presented at the 58th International Communication Association, San Francisco.
Consalvo, M. (2007). *Cheating: Gaining Advantage in Videogames*. Cambridge, MA: MIT Press.

Cova, B., & Cova, V. (2002). Tribal Marketing: The Tribalisation of Society and Its Impact in the Conduct of Marketing. *European Journal of Marketing, 36*, 595–620.

Crowston, K., & Howison, J. (2005). The Social Structure of Free and Open Source Software Development. *First Monday, 10*(2), 1–18.

de Nood, D. & Attema, J. (2007). *Residents in Analyse: De feiten over Second Life na de hype.* Retrieved March 16, 2016, from http://docplayer.nl/6257870-Epn-rapport-residents-in-analyse-de-feiten-over-second-life-na-de-hype-den-haag-november-2007-david-de-nood-jelle-attema.html

de Valck, K. (2005). *Virtual Communities of Consumption: Networks of Consumer Knowledge and Companionship.* Unpublished Ph.D., Erasmus University Rotterdam, Rotterdam.

Field, A. (2005). *Discovering Statistics Using SPSS* (2nd ed.). London: Sage.

Griffin, R. (2017). *Management* (12th ed.). Boston: Cengage Learning.

Kozinets, R. V. (1999). E-tribalized Marketing?: The Strategic Implications of Virtual Communities of Consumption. *European Management Journal, 17*(3), 252–264.

Li, C., & Bernoff, J. (2008). *Groundswell: Winning in a World Transformed by Social Technologies.* Boston: Harvard Business Press.

Ondrejka, C. (2007). Collapsing Geography: Second Life, Innovation, and the Future of National Power. *Innovations, 2*(3), 27–54.

Ortiz de Gortari, A. (2007). *Second Life Survey: User Profile for Psychological Engagement & Gambling.* Paper presented at the Virtual 2007 Conference: Interaction, Stockholm.

Rheingold, H. (1993). *The Virtual Community: Homesteading on the Electronic Frontier* (2001 MIT ed.). Cambridge, MA: MIT Press.

Schultheiss, D. (2007). *Long-Term Motivations to Play MMOGs: A Longitudinal Study on Motivations, Experience and Behavior.* Paper presented at the Situated Play Conference (DIGRA), Tokyo.

Sotamaa, O. (2004, September 19–22). *Playing It My Way? Mapping the Modder Agency.* Paper presented at the Internet Research Conference 5.0, University of Sussex.

van der Graaf, S. (2012). Get Organized at Work! A Look Inside the Game Design Process of Valve and Linden Lab. *Bulletin of Science, Technology & Society, 32*(6), 480–488. ISSN 0270-4676.

van der Graaf, S., & Cobarr, G. (2008). The Second Life of Analogue Players in a Digital World. In A. Koohang & K. Harman (Eds.), *Knowledge Management: Research & Applications* (pp. 21–55). Santa Rosa: Informing Science Press.

von Hippel, E. (2005). *Democratizing Innovation*. Cambridge, MA: MIT Press.

Wiertz, C., & de Ruyter, K. (2007). Beyond the Call of Duty: Why Customers Contribute to Firm-Hosted Commercial Online Communities. *Organization Studies, 28*(3), 347–376.

Zittrain, J. (2008). *The Future of the Internet and How to Stop It*. New Haven: Yale University Press.

4

Of Toolkits, Engines and Interfaces

4.1 Design Space

Existing literature provides comprehensive insights about the cultural status of user participation in production practices vis-à-vis the industry, with notable attention to the uncertain status of user participation in terms of play/work boundaries. These lines of investigation, however, do not paint a full picture of the subject. Considering user participation as a practice that is situated within the industry in general, and the developer firm's logic in particular, it is necessary to examine its role in the design and use in underpinning the firm-hosted 3D platform. Within this setting, this chapter uses qualitative data enriched by some quantifiable evidence to shed light on how user participation has been organized by the developer firm. It features certain characteristics unique to Second Life's platform development and usage, as such, influencing design capabilities and (maintaining) certain aesthetic conventions. In doing so, the chapter complements the discussion of the conjunction of Linden Lab's organizational structure and design capabilities, as presented in the previous chapter.

© The Author(s) 2018
S. van der Graaf, *CommODify*, Dynamics of Virtual Work,
DOI 10.1007/978-3-319-61500-4_4

Here, *design space* is taken as the unit of analysis as it shapes (and affects) the labour process of platform development across its boundaries.[1] This design space is where dynamic migrations occur between the developer firm and mod developers. These migrations draw attention to functionalities of the design space (in particular, the toolkit) provided by Linden Lab and the issue of active 'tethering' through creative and interpretative user activities. More specifically, various functional elements of this design space are examined with particular attention to those tools that assist users with different design capabilities (associated with different kinds of user-developed contributions) to use the platform as they wish. Empirical analysis lays the groundwork to investigate practices that connect user participation to opportunities for the firm to learn, and which may benefit the further development of Second Life (see Chap. 5).

Three areas of mod development are presented, distinguished on the micro, meso, and macro levels of Linden Lab's design space, shedding light on the organization of (mostly) technical characteristics that enable and facilitate this user participation. Linden Lab's perspective on particular interactions or norms and values with the design space by means of the toolkit, and on endeavours of mod developers in terms of conveyance and management are empirically investigated. The design space is further linked to the aspect of transferability. Due to the nature of mod development, where content and code are constantly added, removed and changed by both developers and firm, issues of transferability of such changes to other contributors arise. Particular attention is drawn to types of legal contracts employed between firm and users. The combination of these aspects yields insight into the implementation of trajectories of user participation and creativity in Second Life.

What follows next is an investigation of the Second Life platform as a design space and is organized as follows. First, the micro level design space, which is the in-world environment of the Second Life platform, is discussed. This is followed by the 'intermediate' or meso-level design space, referred to as the Second Life Viewer, which connects the user to the platform. On the macro level, the so-called 'underworld' of the platform is discussed, drawing particular attention to open-source initiatives.

4.2   Inside Second Life: Micro-Level Design Space

On a daily basis, hundreds of gigabytes of data are user-created and added to Second Life, tens of millions of scripts are constantly running in-world and over the last few years users roughly redeemed US$60 million from their Second Life businesses.[2] Let's acquire some insight into the inner workings of the 3D interface that facilitate user participation in development practices. About half of the Second Life population has been reported to experiment with the built-in tools and to invest time to learn how to work with the Second Life toolkit (Ondrejka 2007). Warkirby, a user interviewed for this study, describes his experience of getting acquainted with several functionalities of Second Life:

> I've since gone into content creation pretty much full time. This mainly started in the last six months or so, before that I was exploring and learning. [...] I had a little experience with game mods before Second Life, but it was generally my first time at a lot of things. [...] I've learned most of what I know since coming to Second Life. I spent five months studying scripting on and off here.

It takes time to familiarize oneself with the basic controls of one's Second Life avatar. User retention of roughly 10% illustrates that the majority of users does not get through this learning curve. Yet the ones that do, tend to stay. This may be due to some of Linden Lab's (early) choices of formats and methods, which may not have been standard or platform agnostic, for example, developing its own programming language, Linden Scripting Language (LSL). It is therefore possible that participation in Second Life requires a certain flexibility curve that differentiates between learning the tools the 'system way' or wanting the tools to do certain things in your own way. In this context, Second Life users were asked about the attractiveness of Second Life based on the main functionalities of the Viewer's built-in toolkit, guiding users to engage in building, scripting and texturing practices in-world. The findings indicate that more than half of the respondents found the toolkit an appealing factor to participate in Second Life.[3]

This goes particularly for the membership profiles Twinks, Pros and Experience Brokers (see Chap. 3).

But what do Second Life users actually have at their disposal to work with to enhance the platform? In-world access to the built-in toolkit assists users to explore the possibilities of the design space, to have a go at modding on their own or collaborate with others. This first party toolkit enables users to build, script and texture and can be found on the taskbar under 'Tools'. It allows users to produce houses, mountains and so forth that can be shared, moved, copied and sold. It also permits users to generate and apply textures to created objects and the LSL can be used to manage and control behaviour of in-world objects. More specifically, Second Life's design space is developed in such a manner that it allows for 'atomistic creation' (cf. Au 2008) (Fig. 4.1).

The toolset provides a few basic geometric primitives (referred to as 'prims'[4]) that can be used and combined for 3D modelling purposes. In this regard, this build function is similar to other commercial third-party

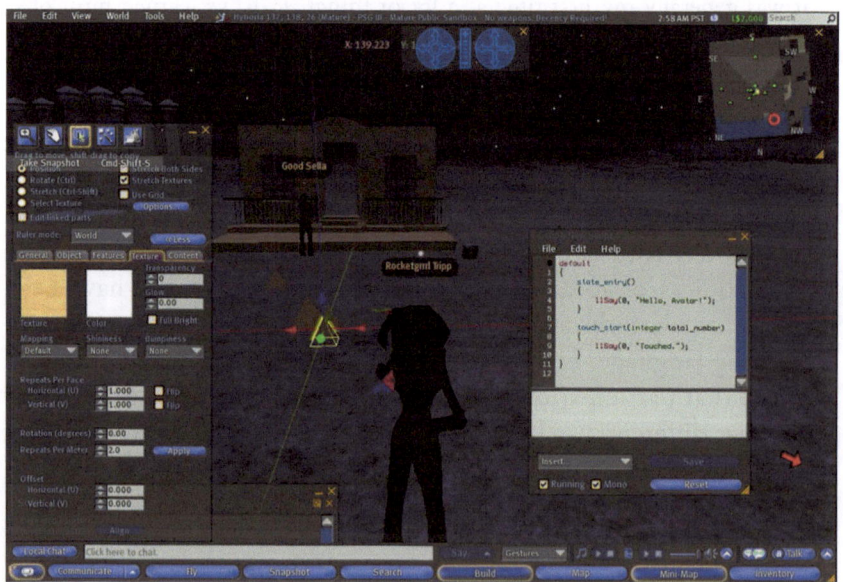

Fig. 4.1 Second life's basic tool palette for building, texturing and scripting (screenshot)

editing tools such as Blender and Maya, but with eight prims it allows less flexible reconfigurations. It enables and facilitates mod developments ranging from simple to complex physical properties and corresponding behaviours. For example, if you were to build a boom box you could do the following: first, select and combine two prims 'box' and 'cylinder' from the built-in toolkit. The prims can be modified in scale, colour, texture and so forth. A sample of Internet radio can be added. And, with the right script (which is a particular piece of source code attached to an object providing and executing behaviour) the boom box can be made to dance through space. In addition, it is possible to make copies of the boom box available for others, freely or for purchase, and when the boom box has served its purpose you could store it in your inventory or you could completely remove it from the platform. The survey asked respondents about their involvement in in-world building practices. The findings indicated that 56% of users frequently participate in building activities.

In-world generated builds can be textured. These textures cannot be made inside Second Life with the exception of several prefab textures provided by Linden Lab in the user's in-world inventory. There are numerous commercial (and free) third-party tools such as Gimp and Texture Makes that can be used to create imagery externally, which can then be imported as a simple image and applied to a single surface. Textures can be seen on objects, like paint, or they can be made transparent ('alpha mapping'). Roughly one-third of the respondents were found to create and import textures. Pros, Power Rezzers and Experience Brokers in particular have an interest in texturing practices.

Scripting using LSL is the internal event-driven, C/Java-style language used to create and control interactivity, run animations, operate gesture poses and so on. The built-in toolkit enables scripts to be written so that they can be placed inside primitive objects.[5] As there are aspects of LSL such as 'HTTP request' that communicate to external web sources, the survey made a distinction between 'script internal' and 'script external', however, for the purpose of this analysis a new variable was created that combined the two scripting variables.[6] Fewer than 20% of the respondents, especially Twinks and Pros, reported to participate in scripting activities, indicating that scripting is a more advanced practice, requiring different skills than for building and/or texturing practices.

In principle, every user that joins Second Life has the capacity to participate in building, texturing and scripting the 3D environment, as it is not a prerequisite to own or rent land. In practice, this means mod development is very much a location-based ability. For example, sandboxes provided by Linden Lab are designated public spaces where anyone can explore, experiment and indulge in tinkering practices. There are some restrictions; objects may not be sold or advertised and a few times per day, sandboxes are cleared out. Having access to land is therefore preferred for more dedicated (and permanent) modding plans. Land ownership permits all sorts of enhancements of the space and, if desired, other users can be invited to participate in modifying land. Different types of land ownership, however, come with variations in toolkit functionality; for example, the simulator (also referred to as 'sim' or 'region') owner has access to all land tools in contrast to the estate manager of a simulator and the land owner within a simulator.[7] The latter has no access to region tools, while the estate manager cannot use terraforming tools (required for loading a raw image file)[8] nor can s/he use server functions such as, rebooting the sim. The estate management tools can thus be fully used by the sim owner and, to some degree, by the estate manager.[9]

There are numerous other in-world design attributes associated with the built-in toolkit that shape (and restrict) the range of user outputs of mod development practices.[10] For example, a teenage participant illustrates such a nuisance.

> Like I have to, I will take a picture of two prims together so it looks like one on Photoshop. I mean, that is really good that I can do that but it would be nice if I could actually show the prim getting shaded by the actual Second Life engine. I mean, there is just so many things like that. (Mike, Teen Grid)

Several other (mostly technical) limitations define the workspace that underlies opportunities for mod development, among which the following are most important. Primitive objects cannot be greater than 10 meters, a complex object cannot link more than 255 prims, a 'link set' cannot exceed 40 meters in any direction, and any kind of vehicle is not allowed to exceed 31 prims. More importantly, sims (regardless of their location on the mainland or island) are always 256 by 256 meters on a side and 65,536 square meters in total. Standard sims cannot have more than 15,000 prims in which to build or handle more than 40 avatars simultaneously.[11] The mainland and islands are always surrounded by water ('ocean') that is 20 meters in depth. Building in a range of 138–248 meters in altitude is subject to frequent cloud formations disrupting visibility. And, lastly, both the centre of an object and land are not allowed to exceed 768 meters in elevation.

In sum, the built-in toolkit conditions the creative space for internal mod development. The next section draws attention to the intermediate or meso-level mod development of the design space, highlighting the Second Life Viewer.

4.3   Accessing Second Life: Meso-Level Design Space

Everyone can download and install Second Life for free. Client software is needed to connect to the servers on which Second Life runs.[12] This software is referred to as the Second Life Viewer (or, 'Client') and is, in its execution, similar to, other real-time 3D rendering engines like the Quake 3 game engine (id Software) or a web-based client like Firefox (Mozilla Corporation). The Viewer is written in C++ and runs on Windows, Macintosh or Linux operating systems. The role of the Viewer is to retrieve, or render, in-world content on the user's computer screen enabling and facilitating the interaction between the user and the platform. Subsequently, the Viewer comes with features that enable users to participate in Second Life including user-to-user interactions (such as via chat, notecards, voice, payments), movement controls (such as walk, fly, teleport); search functionality (such as groups, land sales, world map); community resources (such as abuse, live help, bug reporting, volunteers); and in-world economics (such as buy and sell assets, L$). Moreover, the Viewer fully incorporates the main tools available to all Second Life users that were discussed in the previous section and particular design features such as the appearance mode for avatar customization and terraforming tools for land management.

In addition to the Second Life Viewer, Linden Lab also has provided test Viewers that are indicative of Linden Lab's software release stages.[13] For example, the Release Candidate Viewer is an optional Viewer that includes the latest bug fixes and sometimes also new features that are geared towards a general release. This provides users with an opportunity to learn, explore and test new features and provides Linden Lab with feedback. Beta Viewers do not connect to the Main Grid, but to the Beta Grid. The Beta Grid is a test bed that is open to the general public. All changes made last only for the duration of the session. The Second Life survey also asked respondents about their participation in beta testing. Some 20.5% (N = 429) reported engaging in beta testing activities on a repeated basis. From a closer look at the distribution of responses according to membership profile we can gather that, perhaps unsurprisingly considering their advanced status, the Power Rezzer is most interested in beta testing.

At the beginning of January 2007, Linden Lab added another level to its user participation strategy by releasing the Viewer source code to the public: 'not only can you make things within the world, you can help create future generations of the tool used to interact in-world – the Viewer' (Torley, product manager at Linden Lab, 18/1/07). This intermediate or meso-modding allowed more advanced Second Life users to tinker with the Viewer itself. In fact, from very early on, Linden Lab has been exploring ways to open up, indicating the firm's move towards morphing Second Life into a 3D web environment where users are simultaneously present and connected. Linden Lab saw open-source development as a means to support its plans, affording and sustaining a continuous rapid enhancement of the platform and, hence, for providing even better user experiences. Strictly speaking, Linden Lab recognized that manpower, or the lack thereof, created a bottleneck for further enhancement. Rather than following a linear way of hiring new Lindens, Linden Lab aimed to expand in a non-linear, or boundary-crossing way by inviting mod developers interested in contributing to open source Second Life. Another push came from the community itself, where a group of enthusiasts was working on reverse engineering Second Life, project 'libsecondlife'.

The group built an application that sat between the Viewer and the simulator. As a result, the Viewer would talk to the application that would talk to the Second Life servers. Based on information gathered, the protocol was reverse engineered and mod developers started developing new applications such as CopyBot.[14] Jim explains Linden Lab's choice to open source the Second Life Viewer:

> In some ways open sourcing was inevitable because they were reverse engineering it anyway, and it got to the point where they were building alternative clients to Second Life anyway. And so rather than have a situation where there are two Viewer applications, the open source one and the Linden Lab one, it's far better for everybody that there is an open source version of the Linden Lab code and that people can use that to build alternative clients and then Linden Lab can accept patches to the mainline clients from that alternative version. [...] It's kind of going to happen anyway and also doing it this way means that everybody can potentially benefit from it.

With the release of the Viewer source code several trajectories were developed. The official Viewer was ported and packaged to work with different Linux distributions (with help from volunteer testers that accelerated the process from alpha to beta status). For the atmospheric renderer 'WindLight', originally a proprietary product of which the source code was released in June 2007, Linden Lab received many contributions from mod developers that resulted in a relatively fast track to First Look status. Most contributions, however, are generated in the domain of alternate Viewers. Many are solution-based and of immediate utility as new features may be added, existing ones may be improved, bug fixes may be implemented, and, in some cases, roll back changes may be made (cf. von Hippel 2005). Only a very small percentage of Second Life respondents, in particular the Power Rezzers, reported to tinker with the Viewer, while a large portion has no interest at all in those kinds of practices. Not only individuals but also Second Life-related companies have participated in modding viewers. For example, the OnRez Viewer was a commercially licensed Viewer, developed by TESC and released around the TV show CSI: New York.[15]

4.4 The Underworld: Macro-Level Design Space

During 2007, Linden Lab, by and large, concentrated on upgrading and upscaling aspects of the underlying technology, or 'underworld', of Second Life, which interacts with the Viewer. This was the case due to concerns about scalability, performance and usability. In particular, Linden Lab worked on re-engineering back end systems to transform its APIs into modular and secure web services; upgraded to the Havok engine; and implemented Mono to improve the performance of LSL scripts (and later also other programming languages). By working through these issues, among others, Linden Lab aimed to move towards becoming the market leader in the 3D Internet space. Open-sourcing the servers was an important aspect of this process and intended to signify the move from one grid to multiple grids, that is from a closed to an open system. Yet the stability project seemed to hold up Linden Lab's open-source process as Q, a senior engineer at Linden Lab, explains:

> There's the rub. Right now, we're drastically changing our processes to improve internal stability. A side-effect of that has reduced our ability to accept those kinds of patches. We have enough trouble internally right now. BUT... it's an explicit goal of mine this quarter to help us get to the point of being better able to do that. I'm actually planning to try to do one of my projects outside the firewall so that people can participate and so that I can understand the pain, and hopefully start to address it.

Another reason for a slow open source progress may be found in the platform's monolithic design and trust issues between components that need to be solved in order to prevent undesirable practices among users once all of Second Life is open-source. Furthermore, in the early days, there was no external writable repository. Despite these significant shortcomings, Linden Lab's developers' mailing list (SLDev) showed a steadily growing group of subscribers and developers contributing patches that were rolled in. Yet, the open-source element of Second Life is not the most important draw for people to join Second Life. Only 2% of the respondents reported contributing to open-source activities surrounding the platform on a repeated basis. Considering the advanced skills and know-how level needed to contribute, this small percentage of respondents is consistent with findings of existing studies in the context of user-centred innovation studies.

Throughout the platform's existence, mod development on the micro level has occurred much more often than the incidental projects occurring on macro level design space of the Second Life infrastructure. However, there are several open-source initiatives that, to some extent, interact with Linden Lab, and which are the most advanced forms of user participation. In fact, Linden Lab interviewees claimed to benefit from the active involvement of open-source developers, which seems to fit the presentation of Linden Lab and Second Life as a bottom-up and distributed entrepreneurial system. To this end, Lindens participate in various third-party projects, donate internal source code and have actively sought to work with external parties such as via its Architecture Working Group (AWG) to collaboratively work on scalability and interoperability aspects of the 3D platform. The aim was to define an open protocol that can be standardized. In other words, it allows developers to implement components informing interactions and write their own servers.

AWG was a mixture of Lindens and mod developers. The group organized about four annual meetings and a 'tech-talk' twice a week at then director of Linden Lab's Icehouse Studio, Zero Linden's in-world office. The group used the SLDev mailing list, IRC and a wiki to document its mission by providing an agenda and transcripts, design documents and other resources. The meetings were mainly used for discussing and organizing work, while documentation was developed in the user space and wiki before being released in the main (locked) pages (after within-group consultation and assessment). Furthermore, AWG housed some smaller groups such as Viewpoint Advocacy Groups that tackled specific ideas and issues on a smaller scale and an unofficial user-mod group AW Groupies, consisting of nine core members, also participated in AWG. The operation of AWG has not been entirely positive as indicated by several user-side interviewees.

AWG is a bit bogged down at [the moment] IMO. Seems we are discussing the same things ^^; I think part of the problem is that some people just don't have the technical background for it. It is a very nerdy topic. (Strife)

The thing is if [Zero] is the only one working on that stuff then that might be a problem too. So, he now changed positions somehow. [...] So he might have more time for it now but still it's – I mean there should be more people there. [...] And, I mean in the end, it should be one mailing list for everything and not one internal and one external. [...] I don't see that problem in the end because if we really do that stuff with the old protocol, then at some point, we might not need Linden Lab anymore [...]. (Christian)

Another initiative, founded by the user MW in January 2007 (and is still running), was the project OpenSimulator (or, 'OpenSim') that focused on interoperability. The group consisted of about fifteen core developers and about forty additional developers, testers and other contributors. Many were motivated to contribute to OpenSim as a means to become independent of Linden Lab for reasons that particularly concerned social and technical aspects. More specifically, the developers collaborated to create a common 3D platform (or, 'Virtual Worlds Server') that could be used to develop 3D environments. In practice, this meant that OpenSim allowed the server to connect to any Viewer and vice versa, similar to a browser like Firefox that can connect to the Apache server. Second Life was implemented as its first compatibility project. One contributor hails the project's popularity:

More and more people are joining. This thing is just so amazingly popular that it's incredible. I would never have guessed that about any software project, actually. It seems like people and companies are really interested in spending time on this, so we actually have a lot of companies who are dedicating resources for giving us programming. (Tedd)

For example, IBM made one full-time programmer available and 3Di, the Japanese developer firm of the virtual world platform Jin-sei, provided three programmers who contributed to OpenSim. As a result, most of the code has been donated but, for mostly commercial reasons, participating programmers from developer firms tend to keep back some of the code. OpenSim has received mixed reviews from Linden Lab ranging from disinterest, to bad-mouthing, to respect and lively discussions.

Overall, the empirical investigation has shown that all sorts of contributions can be made to enhance the firm-hosted platform varying from in-world building, to beta testing, to modding the Viewer, to building a server or even an engine from scratch. The three levels of design space functionalities and related opportunities for mod development associated with particular design capabilities discussed above draw attention to the boundaries of Linden Lab. In particular, the ways Linden Lab has sought to manage different creative and interpretative in/outputs of mod developers. This aspect is discussed next with respect to the issue of transferability.

4.5   Servicing Second Life

Time and other investments users make in mod development endeavours can have extensive social and economic connections to the real world. In particular, the many approaches users have taken to engage in creating experiences, mod development practices and, in several cases, generating first-world benefits and/or profits have been discussed previously. Although the results of the empirical investigation indicated that making money was not a strong motivation for respondents to participate in Second Life, the internal economy does appear to affect users in sometimes in small, sometimes in powerful ways.

Money is not per se needed to participate in or have a Second Life, yet even the most basic experience is likely to include the exchange of L$ such as purchasing in-world assets like clothes from others or paying a small fee to bring external assets such as images, sounds and animations in-world. The supply of those assets tends to be produced by Second Life users rather than by Linden Lab. Some mod developers choose to provide their creations (and skills) gratis, while others do charge a fee to earn an income through mod development. How are commercial endeavours of mod developers regarded by Linden Lab? The built-in functionalities provide leverage for the micro, meso and macro levels of the design space, but how are they conveyed and managed with particular attention to IP rights?

Linden Lab defines its own role as provider of a multiuser online service offered through the Linden Software, encompassing Second Life servers, Viewer, APIs and web sites. Linden Lab monetizes its software as a service (SaaS) by providing the software platform for free, while charging according to particular usage patterns. This underlies the firm's aim to refrain from micro-managing in-world interactions between users. Approaching Second Life as a product (and the L$ as part of the package) was consistent with Linden Lab's prominent step in 2003 to give users ownership over their contributions. The survey reported that about two-thirds of Second Life respondents strongly agreed with the statement that holding ownership through IP rights over one's developments was a factor in participating in Second Life.[16]

In the context of IP rights, transferability of mod development is played out differently on the micro, meso and macro levels. Micro-level management influences in-world user endeavours that are interpreted and legally bound by Linden Lab's binding Terms of Service (ToS). The ToS describes services and content of Second Life, user conduct and terms of ownership. The user is given a 'nonexclusive, non-transferable, non-sublicensable, limited, personal and revocable' license to use the software according to the ToS.[17] Participating in mod development (by means of creating or uploading) does not make you 'our employee and you have no rights to compensation.'[18]

Ownership means that users retain IP rights to their creations. Yet, as soon as creations have made it onto the Linden Software, Linden Lab is permitted 'non-exclusive, worldwide, royalty-free, sublicensable and transferable license' to cost-free use and reproduce, distribute, prepare derivative works of, display, perform and so forth, the content throughout its service and for other publicity purposes.[19] Linden Lab reserves the right to delete content without any obligation or liability to the user and it can use generated content for debugging, testing and/or providing support services as it sees fit. Furthermore, it is stated that the user has no data ownership, meaning that, intellectual property rights do not confer any rights of access to the Service or any rights to data stored by or on behalf of Linden Lab. In return, for the duration of the account, a license is granted to use environmental content and textures for development purposes. Users also have to comply with Linden Lab's Trademark Policy as a means to differentiate user contributions from Linden Lab's endorsements.

At the micro level, governance mechanisms have been put in place, ruling over Second Life users that violate another mod developer's copyright. There are various ways, for example, to copy someone else's work and all are considered a breach of the ToS. Copying does not necessarily equal theft, however. Rather, in many on- and offline cases norms have come into existence concerning fair use. An examination of the evolution of community attitudes toward copyright and fair use has shown that historically, media consumers have considered small scale sharing of, for example, music with friends and family as a fair use of content they purchase. However, consumers were also found to harbour strong norms against large-scale copying and/or selling of media (Gasser and Ernst 2006). These norms of sharing have expanded with new technologies, allowing users to engage in seemingly victimless, communal behaviour of sharing their media with others on a larger scale.[20] This may also hold for Second Life. As such, several features have been put in place such as the possibility to use Creative Common licenses and ban lists. Linden Lab states, however, that it is not them but the users who are enforcers of copyright. Users 'grant us the right to protect and enforce our rights to your User Content, including by bringing and controlling actions in your name and on your behalf.'[21] Furthermore, a mod developer can also choose to respond to an alleged copyright infringement by means of the first-world legal system, that is, in accordance with the US Digital Millennium Copyright Act (DMCA). This means that upon receipt of a valid DCMA notification Linden Lab, as service provider, can take down the copyrighted material. The owner is notified so that s/he can file a counter-notification, which may lead to Linden Lab restoring the content.[22]

Meso-level management defines boundaries between Linden Lab and mod developers concerning interface modding of the Second Life Viewer. Contributions are made under the GNU Lesser General Public License version 2.1.[23] This allows mod developers to copy, distribute and modify the Viewer software under the condition that the newly derived result is bound by the same LGPL and, more importantly, that certain libraries can be linked into linking those libraries into non-free programmes. As such, Linden Lab can impose some restrictions. It is possible that in order to develop some derivative mods based on the Viewer software GPL-incompatible libraries may be used. Upon submission of any type of contribution the Second Life Viewer Agreement has to be signed. This document offers joint owner-ship with Linden Lab. More specifically, Linden Lab can 'register a copyright in Your Contribution' and 'exercise all rights as a copyright owner of Your Contribution.'[24] Thus, Linden Lab can (commercially) re-license a mod developer's contribution. In case a mod developer is interested in modding the Viewer software for commercial purposes, s/he cannot use this license. Instead, Linden Lab provides a commer-cial Viewer license that does allow the Viewer to be modded and used proprietarily.

Strictly speaking, there is no licensing for macro-level modding as the Linden servers have not been formally open-sourced. However, as was mentioned earlier, there are several developer groups that contribute to open sourcing the Second Life underworld. OpenSim, for example, makes use of a Berkeley Software Distribution (BSD) license. As the BSD license is more permissive than the GPL,

> people that work on OpenSim are not supposed to be working on the Viewer. We're not even supposed to look at it. Really. Because if we look at it, and we know too much about it, there is a fear that we might acciden-tally steal some of the code and be accused of that [...]. So there's a concern about keeping that separate. Which means, since we're not building the Viewer, we want to remain compatible with Linden Lab. (Dan)

Against this backdrop, Linden Lab's commitment to its aim to become the embodiment of the future of the Internet remains to be seen. The firm's reliance on user input in platform, or product development may be a core capability, but the road to a fully open and decentralized platform by the incorporation of standardized open devices, systems, protocols and servers seems long and winding. Based on the analysis of functional-ities of the design space, the state of user participation on the firm-hosted platform suggests that Second Life operates mainly under Linden Lab's direction and efforts to open up seem to have had a rather closing down implication instead.

4.6   Conclusion: Performative, Iterated and Contextual Mod Development

In this chapter, attention has been drawn to the design space of the firm-hosted 3D platform, to contribute a systematically developed and dynamic approach in building an understanding of the firm-hosted 3D site where user participation is central to design, development and maintenance of the product across firm boundaries. Analysis of design functionalities yielded three loci of user-driven design, which were discussed particularly in terms of leverage, accessibility and transferability.

First, the micro-level design space was introduced. The empirical analysis of micro mod development concentrated on the built-in toolkit that enables and facilitates building, texturing and scripting practices. Based on the outcome of the survey analysis, most respondents engaged in building activities, followed by texturing and, lastly, by scripting. Mod developers are engaged in performative mod development because this in-world development practice is an instance of showcasing that tends to occur 'there and then' in the 3D space, often for others to see.

Second, assessment of the meso-level design space yielded insight into the usefulness of several additional features that service mod development such as terraforming. More importantly, meso mod development addressed a first-level advancement of user participation in mod development, namely, what I refer to as iterated mod development of the Second Life Viewer, which constitutes the client-side of the Second Life platform. Part of the rationale behind the firm's open-source strategy was explained by the firm's need to be able to compete in a 'network effects' market. Another reason was a combination of factors related to within-firm shortage of resources and external reverse-engineering initiatives.

Third, the analysis described the macro-level design space focusing on the platform's underlying technologies and the issue of open sourcing Linden Software's back-end servers. In this context, Linden Lab launched the AWG, a collective of Lindens and mod developers that joined forces to work on a common goal suggesting a convergence of design norms between developer firm and mod developers. Furthermore, despite the fact that Linden Lab has not released this part of the source code, several external developer groups have engaged in what I refer to as contextual mod development, which is a second-level advancement of user participation in mod development. Those initiatives, such as OpenSim, have tended to work on reverse-engineering Second Life and developing external servers to connect to the Second Life grid. As a result, this type of mod development can be said to have overcome or transgressed the limitations of the firm-hosted design space.

How do these findings relate to those concerning design capabilities presented in Chap. 3? Six Second Life memberships based on participation patterns were set out. Based on those findings, Pros, Facilitators and Experience Brokers invest in micro mod development, the Newbs move on the periphery of the micro-level design space and, in particular, the Twinks and Power Rezzers engage in open-source practices of meso and macro mod development. Contributions in the domain of alternate Viewers and the underworld tend to be solution-based and more needs-related, which may point to a more advanced user participant (cf. 'lead mod developer') who is likely to emerge especially from the Power Rezzer category. A synthesized structure of design capabilities in relation to the design space is presented in Fig. 4.2.

The firm-hosted 3D collaborative platform is thus purposefully modular in design (compare also the software release stages of, for example, Release Candidate, First Look and Beta Viewers) allowing enhancement or furthering of parts of the product development process across firm boundaries with no (or minimum) disruption of overall services. The analysis of conveyance and management of this modular design space drew attention to several legal contracts underpinning legally established design limits. Whereas the micro-level design space is managed by a ToS agreement and the meso-level design space is bound by the GNU LGPLv2.1, the findings show that, in practice, there seems to be only a small difference between micro and meso areas of mod development.

On the micro level, mod developers own what they create and make money with it, yet it is developed within the confines of the design space and toolsets and bound by the specifications of the ToS. Overall, there is no 'transferring' to other platforms and only a limited option to 'bring in' various desired features and assets from third-party software packages.

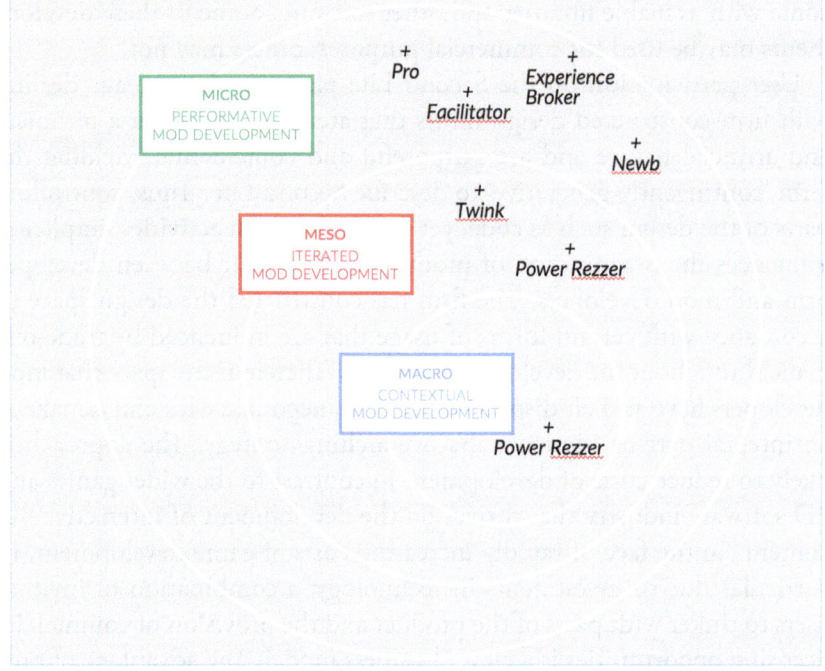

Fig. 4.2 Synthesis of design capabilities and design space

Furthermore, mod developers at the meso level, in contrast to commercial Viewer licensees, are not allowed to derive direct monetary value from their contributions. Therefore, meso-developed mods are, in principle, non-market productions and mainly depend on Linden Lab's proprietary code. Moreover, mod developers seem to find themselves in the peculiar situation of being in the business of creating proprietary experiences (bound by Linden Lab's software) that can be commercial and non-commercial proprietary extensions of the firm-hosted 3D product. For example, explicitly, users can develop in-world digital developments that can be exchanged for money and a commercial Viewer license can be retrieved for business purposes but, implicitly, a freely available user-modded Viewer may result in an overall better Second Life experience and direct more traffic towards the platform. In the case of macro mod development, contracts are dependent on the group licenses that come with available libraries and other software. Some of these developments may be used for commercial purposes, others may not.

User participation on the Second Life platform then means dealing with firm-constructed design limits that are, to a degree, of a technical and artificial nature and are purposeful and coincidental, yielding the term 'contingently generative' to describe Second Life. Thus, controlling parts of the design such as code, yet not the creation activities, implicitly influences the organization of product development between developer firm and mod developers. The firm has constructed the design space in accordance with certain forms of usage that are influenced by trade-offs made throughout the development process. Therein is the space that mod developers have at their disposal to work in, negotiate with and remake as an integral part of Linden Lab's overarching strategy. The approach is likely to reduce costs of development in contrast to the wider games and 3D software industry that thrives on the development of interactive 3D content. In the face of rapidly increasing costs of game development, in particular due to investments in technology, a combination of inviting users to tinker with parts of the product and the provision of commercial licensing opportunities is a clever business model. The advantage of providing a multilevelled design space as a platform for a range of user participation practices is that it favours creative capacities of users over having them concentrating on the mechanics.

On the basis of the analysis so far, however, a more critical engagement with the conceptualization of user participation seems desirable, in particular with regard to variable degrees to which mods appear to be easily transferable (in-world transferability among users and/or the firm seems the most straightforward). More specifically, design functionalities on the level of the design space seem to indicate a type of (temporary) role-based coordination of different levels of mod development that furthers various aspects of product development. This may yet have implications for the extent of participatory opportunities, the exchange of knowledge between projects and more. The next chapter further assesses the role of users on the firm-hosted platform by empirically investigating the ways dynamic relationships between users and the developer firm are developed and organized with the aim of highlighting learning opportunities for the developer firm.

Notes

1. The design space for mod development is not viewed as technologically deterministic; rather as a process of reciprocal interaction of the space and/or the tools with contributing developers, which unfolds in networked constellations of practices (NcoP).
2. See Linden Lab's CEO Ebbe Altberg at https://www.youtube.com/watch?v=6cDXvZUFmTU (accessed 22/12/16). Note that in 2007, its heyday, there were roughly 100 million database queries each day, 50 terabytes of user-created data and 26 million peer-to-peer transactions (Presentation 'Continual Opening of Second Life' by R. Lanphier and A. Brashears at O'Reilly Open Source Convention, Portland, 27 July 2007).
3. See http://etheses.lse.ac.uk/100/ for all statistical information used in this book (in particular, Chap. 6).
4. There are eight prims that can be used for building purposes: box, cylinder, prism, sphere, torus, tube, ring and sculpted prisms. These can be modified in terms of size, cut, transparency, etc.
5. Note that avatars can only wear scripted objects.
6. Internal scripting refers to particular in-world scripting activities with no connection to external sources, while external scripting refers to scripts that are either in LSL sending messages out or receiving messages from within or, more likely, scripting or coding that is outside Second Life in a web site or other web-based application.
7. Sim is a sim host, or the hardware, a simulator, is the binary that runs on the sim hosts and regions run in the simulator.
8. *Terraforming tools* are land tools that allow the user to raise, lower, flatten and/or smooth the terrain.
9. These tools, however, are more about management and control than about creation, and include functions such as region (e.g., block flying); debugging (e.g., collision); ground textures (e.g., importing images); terrain (e.g., uploading a raw image file); estate (e.g., add and remove estate managers); and, covenant (e.g., define rule sets).
10. Note that in-world one day lasts three hours and the night is only one hour.
11. Typically, one server supports two or more sims.
12. Most of this research was conducted by using version 1.19.1.4.
13. Note that over time Linden Lab's strategy changed from having major point releases (every few months) to more feature-rich releases over a shorter time span.

14. *CopyBot* was a programme that let users copy objects without permission of their creators.
15. Making code accessible also lowers the threshold for third-party companies that are interested in commercial licensing opportunities.
16. Power Rezzers score relatively high on 'strongly disagree' in comparison to other clusters that may be explained by their relative 'outer-platform' interests that are underpinned by different legal contracts.
17. See under §2.2 See: https://www.lindenlab.com/tos (accessed 22/12/16).
18. Ibid §9.5.
19. See under §2.3 and §2.5.
20. This was branded by the media industries as 'theft'.
21. See §2.3.
22. See §7.
23. See http://wiki.secondlife.com/wiki/Linden_Lab_Official:Second_Life_Viewer_Licensing_Program (accessed 22/12/16). The artwork is licensed under the Creative Commons Attribution-Share Alike 3.0 License.
24. See   http://lecs.opensource.secondlife.com/SLVcontribution_agmt.pdf (accessed 22/12/16).

References

Au, W. J. (2008). *The Making of Second Life: Notes from the New World*. New York: HarperCollins.

Gasser, U., & Ernst, S. (2006). *From Shakespeare to DJ Danger Mouse: A Quick Look at Copyright and User Creativity in the Digital Age*. Retrieved February 15, 2015, from https://cyber.harvard.edu/publications/2006/From_Shakespeare_to_DJ_Danger_Mouse

Ondrejka, C. (2007). Collapsing Geography: Second Life, Innovation, and the Future of National Power. *Innovations, 2*(3), 27–54.

von Hippel, E. (2005). *Democratizing Innovation*. Cambridge, MA: MIT Press.

5

Learning and the Imperative of Production in Mod Development

5.1 Learning by Design

Digital firms, in particular, can be seen to increasingly invite, host and make use of online user communities on their platforms. This is the case because those communities provide an unprecedented capability as information resources, underpinning, for example, feedback and problem-solving mechanisms. Research findings have, so far, insufficiently addressed the systematic role of these firms in the context of user participation, although they seem to demonstrate a shift from 'firms as producers' to 'firms as platform (or, service) providers'. Instead, studies have often focused on the practices themselves and, in many cases, on not-for-profit or 'commons'-oriented platforms such as various open-source communities.

This chapter links the design capabilities and the design space to knowledge contribution practices of users and Linden Lab employees alike, highlighting aspects of learning (within and) across firm boundaries that underpin product development practices on the firm-hosted 3D platform. Particular attention is directed at informational inputs in the context of product development that may stem from within and external sources of the developer firm that highlight the ways (shared) practices and platform use may generate opportunities for individual and

© The Author(s) 2018   **113**
S. van der Graaf, *ComMODify*, Dynamics of Virtual Work,
DOI 10.1007/978-3-319-61500-4_5

collective development to occur. This strategy of consulting with the user positions the Second Life platform, at baseline, as a site where ideas about discovering, developing and refining modifications are provided by both the developer firm and mod developers. In this view, the investigation seeks to illuminate the extent of cross-pollination among different users and the developer firm. In doing so, aspects of mastery and apprenticeship are investigated, which signal particular knowledge loci that may be connected to various firm-user learning prospects. In this relational approach mod development is understood as a *learning dynamic* and in this capacity serves here as the unit of analysis.

What follows next is an analysis of the relational and underlying dimension of mod development as a learning dynamic. Attention is drawn to the means of information retrieval and supply by Second Life users. This is followed by examining learning practices taking place on the micro, meso and macro design space, and the implications for firm-user learning opportunities occurring as a catalyst of product development. In particular, mastery and leadership practices are highlighted. The findings draw attention to the centripetal effect of complex and crossover learning that may particularly benefit the firm, exposing the firm's fundamental challenge of integrating and learning from users' shared input and contributions.

5.2   Mod Development as a Learning Dynamic

In order to conceptualize user participation in development practices as a learning dynamic on the firm-hosted platform key factors need to be identified. This is achieved by examining how users establish and renew relations with each other, and understanding the underlying structure of information and communication practices among Second Life users. For this purpose, the survey on Second Life was used to learn about communication patterns and served as input for a Principal Component Analysis to reveal existing linear components in the data set and the way specific variables contribute to that component (Field 2005).[1]

Respondents were asked about frequency of retrieving and supplying information on channels provided by Linden Lab; the Official Second

Life Blog, Second Life forums, scripters mailing list, SLDev mailing list, open-source portal (or, wiki), LSL portal (or wiki) and in-world group messages.[2] The results show that in-world messaging, the blog and forums are frequented most often. Furthermore, based on the respondents (N = 434) that supplied information, 37.1% reported to typically reply more to posts than to initiate posts. This is followed by 29.5% of the respondents who said they retrieve and supply a similar number of messages. Only 8.5% post more than they retrieve information, while 4.4% only reply to other people's posts and 1.2% only retrieve information without supplying it. This is further investigated in the next section concerning firm-user learning.

Respondents were also asked to rank their preferred means of communication to find out how to do certain things in Second Life. The Official Linden Lab Blog (and archives) is deemed most important, closely followed by the Second Life Forums (and archives), Member-owned external URLs, the Knowledge Base and LSL Portal, while the Open Source Portal and Contact support (email, phone) are valued by less respondents. Interestingly, external sites hosted by other Second Life users ranked quite well, that is, before the firm-provided knowledge base and even support. Further examination shows that more than half of the respondents (57.8%, N = 429) reported that they have engaged in activities that concern and promote Second Life externally such as on user-run blogs and web sites. In addition, nearly 40% (N = 428) reported to have posted Second Life-related information on web sites like YouTube and Flickr. It is therefore likely that many of those sites offer useful and qualitative resources.

In order to delve deeper into communication patterns the survey a Principal Component Analysis was conducted. Questions with a five-point rating scale were asked about the appeal of Second Life; usage and usefulness of various firm-provided tools and features of the platform; participation in information and communication activities; orientation towards others ('other-directedness'); and several of Linden Lab's services. Examples of these items included, respectively: 'I can enjoy social interactions with others'; 'Do you mod the Viewer source code?'; 'How useful is the Linden Scripting Language for you?'; 'Do you post Second Life-related information on sites like YouTube,

Flickr, and Del.icio.us?'; 'How often do you read the Official Linden Blog?'; 'How often do you post or comment on the SLDevelopers mailing list?'; 'How often do companies ask you to develop their presence in-world?'; and, 'How would you rate Linden Lab's response to feature and development requests?'

This resulted in eight factors.[3] The first factor, meta (17.41% of variance, .880 Cronbach's α),[4] refers to advanced and specific links of communication and adoption behaviour. It contains those questions that loaded highly on open-source practices, the retrieval and supply of information about open source, developers and scripters mailing lists, LSL, hacking activities and interest generation from companies. Meta measures high-end usage of the platform that may be related to the macro and meso level of mod development. The second label *scripting* (8.98% of variance, .901 Cronbach's α) measures moderate to advanced capabilities and usage of the design space that may be associated with scripting practices. The items that loaded highly were the retrieval of information about open source, LSL and the scripters mailing list, participation in scripting activities (such as vehicles and physics, and in-world games), beta tests, and JIRA.

In-world orientation (6.82% of variance, .895 Cronbach's α) combines items that are directed towards micro-level mod development. In particular, aspects of information and communication were related to questions that asked about posting and commenting to the blog, in-world group messages and the forums. Furthermore, elements of in-world improvement are user-to-user- and user-to-firm-oriented by helping others, validated opinions, bug submissions, JIRA and beta tests. The questions that loaded onto the factor building and texturing (4.77% of variance, .850 Cronbach's α) measure in-world usage of build and texture activities indicating micro-level mod development. It combined the items related to 'enjoy participating in said practices' that may have included, among other entities, producing artwork, clothes and fashion.

Organizational character (3.54% of variance, .835 Cronbach's α) measures the construct referring to the services provided by Linden Lab. Respectively, the developer firm's responses to customer service, technical issues, community feedback, abuse, features and development requests, and purchase and billing information. The sixth factor measures the features (3.39% of variance, .843 Cronbach's α) that support in-world mod development such as animations, appearance editor, inventory and uploading and file format. The factor other-directedness (3.19% of variance, .858 Cronbach's α) measures the orientation of users towards others. Questions that loaded strongly on this factor were related to helping others (other users and companies alike), opinion leadership and engaging in communicative activities concerning Second Life on external platforms. The last factor reveals the underlying structure of items that measure Second Life's perceived innovative character (2.58% of variance, .849 Cronbach's α). It combined the items of retaining IP rights, hacking, open-source modifications and the features sculptable primitives and XML.

By simplifying the data based on respondents' responses, the underlying structure revealed that especially the factors meta, scripting, in-world orientation and other-directedness measure communicative elements.[5] The meta construct that embraces communication means concerns the more advanced topics of mod development. Scripting scores considerably lower on the retrieval of information than the meta factor, while knowledge contributions are, in comparison to meta, virtually absent. The in-world orientation component measures the retrieval and supply of information of the blog, forums and in-world group messaging. Other-directedness contains items involving the supply of Second Life-related information via external web sites and so forth. Against this information and communication framework, a closer examination of user participation vis-à-vis firm-user learning can be interpreted and is discussed next.

5.3 Mastering Second Life: The Developer Firm's Perspective

What follows is an attempt to expose various aspects of the organization and implications of crossover practices for firm-user learning by examining the internal enculturation practices within Linden Lab. In particular, apprenticeship and knowledge-sharing practices are addressed.

Previously in this book, Linden Lab's rather extensive distributed decision-making policy was highlighted associated with an entrepreneurial attitude as a criterion for getting a job. Pivotal in this regard is that Lindens can choose what (not) to work on, and that a Linden's success or failure is very much connected to not only executing tasks well, but also communicating them well to others to make them understand the value of those tasks (hence, the role of the Linden). If a Linden cannot do a task on her own, they should find a team or, if they potentially need someone with more experience in an area, they are encouraged to find someone who wants to teach them. This is, however, not to say that Linden Lab is completely devoid of a type of seniority system. Lindens can take on extra responsibilities such as mentoring newbies to guide them into the 'Linden way' and chart their careers. Brett recalls his first week at Linden Lab:

> There's a steep learning curve for people that first come into the company because there's just a lot of specific tool sets, and communication techniques, and things that they prefer that you use to, kind of, get calibrated to the Linden way. [...] I was set up at a desk with a computer. There are two buildings actually right across the street from each other [...] So I made the mistake of assuming that [my first meeting] was a physical meeting because people said "Oh there's a meeting at 3" or whatever time it was. And so I literally scattered and ran across the street to the other building to meet with the Marketing Executive [...] and they look at me like I was crazy. [...] "You can have a meeting in-world."

For a newcomer in any company it may be unclear what the preferred means of communication are. Starting in a company where the choice of work is your own is, according to the Linden interviewees, for many somewhat 'mind-boggling'. The role of the mentor therefore is to guide new Lindens into this process of 'choosing wisely' by having them choose things that can be reasonably achieved and by guiding them in how to manage their work (and, they play also a role in salary reviews). The mentor is particularly important during the first few months 'when you're like figuring out what the hell's going on in this crazy hippyfied company' (Jim 12/1/07). Mentorship, however, is available for the duration of employment at Linden Lab, which is explained by Q, while Torley underscores the possibilities of moving forward internally.

> Everyone is expected to choose a mentor and have regular meetings. Mentorships can change over time as your needs change. My mentor is a program manager, because I wanted someone not in development. Well... that part I've been doing for a while, and I'm one of the more senior devs [developers] around. But everyone needs to hear about how they're doing managing their work, their social interactions, etc. (Q)

> She guides me in my personal and professional development. I show her regular reports of my work and she advises me in areas of improvement, things I should be looking for next. (Torley)

Another illustration of a process that guides internal labour practices is the studio system.[6] The studio is development oriented and headed by a studio director, whose most important task is to oversee and manage multiple projects, not people. Lindens are not attached to a particular studio and, therefore, the director fulfils a kind of guidance and awareness role concerning resource management. This is a rather big challenge as many Lindens have an opinion about what is 'most important' in order to move Second Life forward. A studio is not attributed a single work area per se, depending on the studio director, each studio tends to have certain specialisms. For example, a new developer generally spends her or his first few weeks in Studio Blacklight, which concentrates on high priority bugs and issues that affect the service. The focus on solving bugs rather than being project oriented provides an insightful way for newcomers to acclimatize and familiarize themselves with Second Life, its inner working and tasks ahead. After a while, some new developers may become excited by other developments and proceed to another studio.

Note that another common way of organizing the development process is the cabal, a type of temporary role-based coordination among developers. At Valve Inc., for instance, this format tends to represent major technical development groups and consists of eight to twelve people that self-organize. Depending on where they are in the design process the cabal members may sit in the same office, meet once a week, or, for example, when a proposed idea requires more people to work on it gets explored in a temporary mini cabal. In this view, in the cabal members are banded together based on their skills at the time that they are required, and this is guided by the so-called design document (van der Graaf 2012).

For a successful career at Linden Lab, it is important to master the various communication channels, such as Second Life (used for meetings, presentations, etc.) and IRC (used for communicating emergencies, etc.), which are interwoven into Linden Lab's internal organization of labour. JIRA was said to be pivotal in this regard as it manages tasks and projects concerning platform development. More specifically, Lindens use JIRA on a daily basis to submit and retrieve tasks, bugs, for example. It is also a mechanism to prioritize work as once a week issues that are considered worth doing are ranked by votes cast by Lindens. In the words of Jim:

> If you were being completely mechanical about it, one way of working you could choose to do, would be whenever you finish a piece of work, go to JIRA, find the thing with the highest number of votes, so this is the thing that most people in the company think is worth doing, pick it up and do it. And there are some people who kind of work like that. And there are other people who work in particular areas and have a more personal appreciation of what needs to be done and will work on that, and there's a kind of guideline that if you propose a task and it doesn't get any votes, then you should think twice about doing it or ask somebody else about doing it.

JIRA shows what options are available and underscores the interdependence of tasks and goals. As Torley put it, 'I choose my own work – out of a pile that's selected for me in the first place by others, Lindens and Residents!'. Furthermore, projects usually stretch over several months or more, which delicately constrains Lindens from 'pingponging' between various tasks, which could potentially stagnate or even harm product development. JIRA is also used to assess a Linden's performance on, and mastery of, the job. Each quarter every Linden has a review day where accomplishments are gathered from JIRA based on 'As & Os', and the JIRA-modified 'Love Machine'.[7]

JIRA provides general metrics such as what tasks have been accomplished and yields a post-analysis of how things were executed, while the

Love Machine is a more qualitative means of assessment. On a daily basis Lindens give and receive 'love' from their colleagues. In practice this means that when, for example, someone is stuck writing code, s/he can ask for help. In return, a Linden sends out a 'love note' to thank the person who has helped out. The Love Machine is therefore providing insight into which Lindens are helping which other Lindens; this accumulates as a quantifiable value. At the end of each quarter every Linden gets a pink envelope with money in it, as every 'love note' received translates into US$ 1.

Not only is a Linden evaluated based on tasks performed and the extent of peer interactions, the review is also viewed by a number of co-workers and their comments accompany the review as well. In another attempt to achieve transparency, both 'love' scores and reviews are published internally on a wiki for everyone to read. Linden Lab has also been experimenting with a bonus distributor. During a profitable quarter each Linden is given a few 'points' and can decide how s/he wishes to distribute those points among her/his colleagues. This strategy is consistent with Linden Lab's philosophy of remaining as flat an organization as possible by putting compensation distribution into the hands of all Lindens and, therefore, nurturing a culture where employees appear to be empowered to make decisions rather than a concentrated bunch of Linden executives.

All these organizational means are suggestive of Linden Lab's distributed structure that is associated with transparency rather than with more traditional management styles, which are believed by the interviewees to encourage company-wide learning and to underlie creative problem solving.

> [There are] some very smart people and me being mostly non-technical I learn A LOT from the techies. People here are always happy to share knowledge. ... our internal wiki and blogs really encourage it too. (Blue)

5.4 Mastering Second Life: A Mod Developer's Perspective

Let's now take a look at the mechanisms at work that guide mod developers into the 'doings and sayings' of this so-called modification culture. First-time users of Second Life are introduced and mentored by a built-in functionality that automatically directs newcomers to Orientation Island. It is here that they are introduced and guided through the basic controls and functions of, especially, the avatar. However,

> if you have no gaming history you are going to have a much steeper learning curve. Mostly, in regards to controlling your avatar's body and attempting to speak through chat or IM. [...]. You can be made fun of the way you dress or act or what you do not know, especially that. To be labelled a 'newb' or 'noob' is the ultimate put down label. (Garrett)

From Orientation Island the newcomer is transferred to a Welcome Area and left to her or his own devices. There are, however, many resources available that can be tapped that can assist and enhance the experiences of new Second Life users. Examples of such firm-provided resources include in-world workshops and courses, libraries, knowledge base, wiki portals, videos, blog and forums. There are also user contributions that mix with Linden-produced ones. For example, one interviewee volunteered to write most of the LSL content for the Second Life wiki and also moderated several of the Second Life forums. In addition, there are various support channels that correspond to specific account types associated with Second Life membership. For example, a premium account holder can access live chat, while fee-based enterprise level support is serviced 24/7 by a so-called concierge team. There are also many user- and third-party-provided means of support similar to the firm-hosted ones including blogs, forums, wikis, newspapers, instruction guides, videos and podcasts, books and sandboxes.

Not only resources can be consulted; generally other users are friendly and are likely to help out. An adult user describes how he sees his mentoring role:

> I do scripting mentoring, which means I may tell you how to solve your problem, but I won't solve it for you. (Strife)

Consulting with fellow Second Life users seems often to be preferred over Linden Lab's, to various extents, poorly designed documents and support channels, indicating a situation of interdependence between

Linden Lab and its user base. In this context, the survey asked respondents to rank their preferred means of communication to find out how to do particular things in Second Life. By far, the most preferred was to ask someone you know in-world via IM, followed by asking a group in-world or visit an in-world library and another but not so popular pathway could be to ask anyone in-world within visual range via chat, and lastly was to ask a Linden in-world.

Most users work on the micro-level design space, which translates to users that work inside their own project. As a result, most of the development, at least in this sample of users, takes place real-time in-world and, subsequently, it is not unheard of that developers can count on working in front of an audience; hence its designation as performative mod development. Skilled developers can rapidly make shapes appear in space, turn, twist and join them, and change their colour and textures. Such performances are, in many cases, sites for apprenticeship.

> I mean [I learned] some stuff in the forums which I was reading, of course, but mostly it was trying around and meeting people in the sandbox and talking to them and learning maybe a little bit from them or just looking how other people do it and trying to replicate that and then build on this so, learning by doing. (Christian)

Sandboxes, however, are of a temporary character as they are cleared out daily. So if users are interested in pursuing work in-world, buying or renting land becomes necessary. Acquiring land involves familiarizing oneself with various aspects of this mechanism such as tier, number of prims needed and location. It is not uncommon for users to 'learn by doing' and sell off their first land quite rapidly for a more suitable piece that fits their needs better. Neighbours are an important factor in this regard. Neighbours with contrasting goals (think, a gambling palace next to a spiritual and quiet zone) can cause severe distress and lead to security issues and performance lag. Good neighbours with different levels of skills-set and knowledge may revel in offering each other advice and assistance, every now and then, resulting in group initiatives.

Some users are more interested in the technology and the way these applications are used and move towards a 3D web environment, such as mod developers who participate in open-source initiatives. This is mod development occurring on the meso level, that is, user-modded Viewers. Many developers make their code freely available for others to use and mod. In addition, progress and findings are often written down in blog format. Although others can contribute and provide feedback, Viewer modifications tend to be an individual effort (unlike Viewers that are commercially licensed).

Macro mod development, however, is very much a collaborative practice. In reality, mod developers that worked on OpenSim were said not to spend much time using the Second Life platform. Rather they collaborated using IRC, mailing lists and software repositories, thereby differentiating between channels for helping others, for development and for the core group. Logs and word searches assist in keeping track of certain interests. The software repository functions as the repository for the source code and as a bug tracker where bugs or feature requests can be entered and which, in turn, are assigned to someone (or can be chosen to be worked on). When developers add something new or make changes, they add some comments and an overview of what has been done. This is distributed via IRC and the mailing lists so as to ensure all participants are up to date.

> This sort of then brings up a lot of discussion around what just happened and stuff like that, and people, a lot of people on the channel upgrade their servers immediately to try the new features or to test it or stuff like that so we get feedback right away so we can fix the feature if it doesn't work or if something breaks. (Tedd)

Yet, not all mod developers are granted access to write code to the repository. Newcomers may be granted those privileges when they have proven themselves over time in terms of reliability, technology usage (such as IRC) and delivering good work. Holding the position of core developer for that matter is not guaranteed either. When a core member starts investing less time and energy in contributing work, s/he will be replaced:

> There is a person right now who's probably more in touch with what's going on in physics than I am because I've been gone for 3 weeks, pretty

much. And if I want to come back in, now I have to come back in, to some degree I have to prove myself again. Come back in, fix some of his bugs, and help put some features in that weren't there. And then they'll be, "OK, he hasn't lost it," you know, "He still knows what he's talking about." (Dan)

Authority appears to be determined substantially by the ideals of meritocracy. Some developers are likely to be more specialist, while others are more generalist. In addition, there are also tasks that are more of a supportive nature than writing the actual code such as cleaning up the library repository and maintaining the web site. These may be executed by the developers but are more likely to be performed by non-programmers as part of the development group (cf. Berdou 2011). Overall, the mastering of macro mod development of Second Life involves a rather stringent and distributed review process where skills and contributions are constantly confirmed and reconfirmed so as not to compromise the overall project.

5.5   Learning from User Participation

After the 2007 Second Life Community Convention, former CEO Philip Rosedale received 'love' for trying to engage in meaningful conversations with all of the 800 attendants over the course of three days. He included this bit of 'love' in his quarterly review and accompanied it with a note expressing how important it is for Linden Lab to listen to Second Life users. Not all Lindens, however, are likely to possess the same level of awareness, or exposure, and engagement with the user base which, arguably, is directly connected to the area of work they engage in internally. For example, the community team, consisting of about a dozen Lindens, occupy key client-faced roles such as community affairs (such as abuse), and user communication, while areas such as programming deal to a far lesser extent directly with users, which Steve underscores:

When we work on feature development, we are much more involved with communicating with the residents. At the moment I am more focused on stability and performance where the motivation is pretty straightforward – reduce the crash rate and make SL perform better :)

As many Lindens were mere users prior to becoming Linden Lab employees, many have maintained their private accounts to continue their Second Life in that capacity.

Personally I spend quite a lot of time on Second Life, maybe a couple of hours a week, not as a Linden [...]. I think it's valuable to my work but I think it's separate from my work, you know I don't spend my time in Second Life trying to find out where Second Life needs to be improved, but some of the things I do in Second Life make me aware of the things in Second Life that you can change so I think, you know, spending time in Second Life is valuable whether or not you're actually trying to use it as part of your work or not. (Jim)

Regardless of a Linden's individual interaction with users, Linden interviewees uniformly acknowledge the status of Second Life as a development platform that depends on user creativity, social interactions and entrepreneurship. The platform has attracted many smart and skilled users providing useful and helpful contributions that, in many cases, can be beneficial to all. The amount of user-provided information can also become overwhelming (particularly when every user seems to point to a different set of features that are important to her/him). Several Lindens have a day job to filter out input most critical for internal use, to prioritise and communicate it internally. In particular, they dedicate a lot of time interacting with users in order to learn what works well, what the biggest issues are and so forth. In order to listen to its user base, Linden Lab has put in place tools and methods that facilitate and organize the contribution of ideas and feedback by those users interested. The remainder of this section yields insight into the ways those interactions between Linden Lab and mod developers function as learning opportunities underlying mod development.

Blogs, Forums, Mailing Lists and JIRA

There are multiple ways for the developer firm and users to interact and share information. Much of the communication tends to occur on a nearly day-to-day basis, via the blog, in-world office hours, JIRA, mailing lists, wiki and forums. First-life focus groups and design discussions are organized on weekly and quarterly bases. The empirical investigation at hand concentrates mainly on blog, forums, mailing lists and JIRA.

The Official Second Life Blog is considered to be Linden Lab's main communication channel.[8] The Linden interviewees reported reading blog and comments, particularly the ones that pertain to what they are working on or when the post is theirs. Occasionally, they said they contributed posts and comments themselves. The total blog activity was measured between October 2004 and February 2008. It showed that 98 Lindens contributed 1517 posts, 65 Lindens wrote 1592 comments and 21,059 users made 95,252 comments. Further analysis showed that one of the Linden interviewees, Torley, was the main contributor to the blog with 162 posts followed by four colleagues who contributed between 80 and 87 posts. Although the top blogger also received the most comments from the community, the analysis also showed that several less frequent Linden posters received more comments than a few contributors with a higher frequency of posting.

The findings also showed that Lindens do engage with commenters on the blog by reacting on comments. Sidewinder Linden, for example, was not a very active poster but scored just below the top poster/commenter on the number of comments supplied. These comments are very much related to clarification and quality concerns. This should be viewed as a learning dynamic indicative of firm-user interactions. For instance, Sidewinder tends to provide the community with technical status updates such as the usage of the Havok-4-based Second Life simulator in the Beta Viewer and various in-world 'early adopter regions'. In a 147 comment-long thread, troubles are discussed that occurred in areas that worked well prior to the update. The following discussion illustrates that both Linden Lab and mod developers (jointly) attempted to solve the problem:

> [...] I went back to review that bug report, and noticed that there was some internal discussion in the comments that seemed to be about what proper behavior should be, and how to replicate it. I had thought when I last looked at it that our current fixes might make the issue you've reported behave better or even be resolved. Have you checked the behaviors with the code we deployed tonight to see if things are working any better (and if

not, could you check to see if it has been addressed by other work that we have done)? If not, please let me know in-world, and I'd be happy to drop in so that you can demonstrate the problem. Something to note is that we had thinned the physical representation of the avatar somewhat in previous builds, and went back to make it larger again (part of fixing hugger positioning). I wonder if the slender avatar representation was part of what was making it seem that kicks did not work well. /Sidewinder. (blog id 76432)

@22 Sidewinder – The behavior is definitely different now, though not quite correct. Previously a kick against a standing opponent in Havok-4 would do nothing at all, now it does push them just a bit in the air vertically, but with no horizontal movement. I sent you an object that can repro that with just a click, and the script inside is simplified to (hopefully) make it clearer how it was intended to work in HAVOK-1. The other cases mentioned in that JIRA issue in the comments may also be changed, but I've not yet had the chance to find out. (blog id 76475)

Fig. 5.1 presents a tag cloud of the total blog commenters based on the number of comments they have contributed. It shows that a few Lindens score relatively high among user commenters in the contributions they make to the blog. Respectively, Usagi Musashi/U M made 1867 comments, Ann Otoole 767, Argent Stonecutter 479, Torley Linden 402, Lina Pussycat 376, Lewis Nerd 337 and Sidewinder Linden 335.

Fig. 5.1 Blog commenters by comment count (*N* = 22,649)

Second Life forums are another channel for people to connect. Interaction with users in the forums is predominantly the focal point for Linden Lab's community and customer service teams. An important reason for this is related to the volume of forum threads and to a large noise-to-signal ratio that makes it rather time consuming to pick out meaningful and valuable user comments. The Linden interviewees tend to visit the forums in those cases when a colleague has pointed them to a particular topic that s/he should participate in. Their participation is driven by trying to be helpful and informative:

> In the past I would participate in forum discussions, not so much now but still sometimes. Mostly because I'm working too hard. But sometimes I pipe in on some issue on which I have opinions or plans. (Andrew)

A closer look at the forums showed that 149,957 posts and 1,307,814 comments were made between November 2002 and February 2008. A further breakdown showed that 94 Lindens and 24,755 users contributed posts, while 140 Lindens and 30,106 users supplied comments. For this study threads were divided by first post and comments. This was a means of investigating apprenticeship relations and mobilizing leadership by highlighting information retrieval and supply. More specifically, apprenticeship by means of opinion leadership was connected to being knowledgeable about a topic and information sharing (de Valck 2005; Frederiksen 2006). From this viewpoint, leadership is thought to positively affect mod development by offering learning opportunities in firm-user interactions (Morrison et al. 2004). Figure 5.2 yields insight into communication behaviour in Second Life forums. Each dot, representing an individual, shows the total number of initiated posts and the total number of contributed comments. On the far right, Torley Linden out-commented the user base with 14,332 comments (and 230 thread starts), while SuezanneC Baskerville is the top poster among users with 1471 posts (and 7644 comments). Note that most forum contributions concentrate between roughly 150 posts and 1500 comments. Furthermore, forum participants tend to comment more than they start threads and, by and large, outnumber Linden participants.

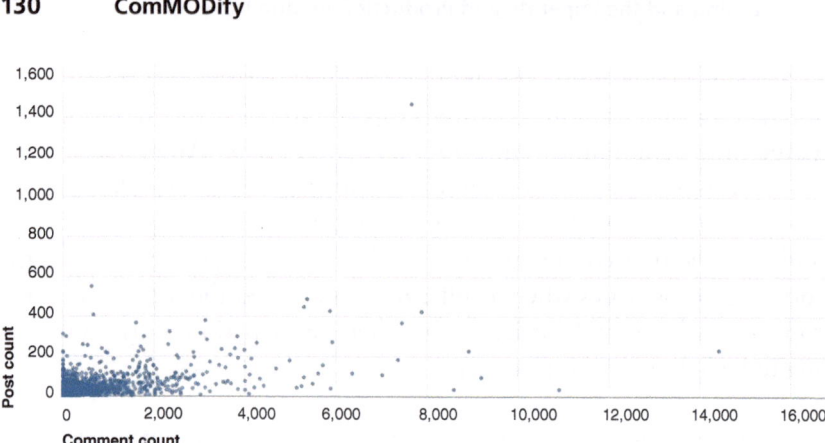

Fig. 5.2 Second life forums: posters vs. commenters

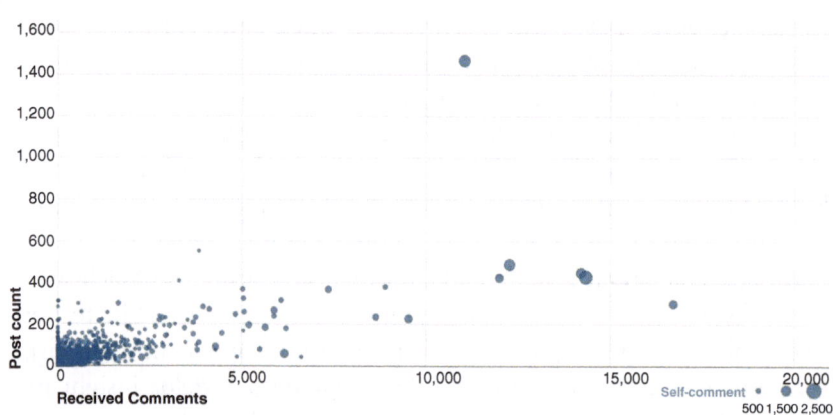

Fig. 5.3 Second life forums: posters by received comments and self-comment behaviour

Figure 5.3 presents the analysis of forum participants according to the total number of posts made, total comments that were received and the number of self-comments that were made on those initiated posts. It shows that only a handful of contributors received a large volume of comments and that those users also scored high on self-commenting activities. In this regard, Lindens scored relatively low.

The Second Life mailing lists cater to specific interest groups. The everyday volume of the developers (SLDev) and scripters lists is experienced as being too high for some of the Linden interviewees to sift through. As a consequence, these emails are filtered into a particular folder for later reading or for deletion. Figure 5.4 shows the key contributors to the developers (left) and scripters mailing lists (right) in terms of who contributes and number of posts.[9] Several Lindens who are interested in open source and other technical topics are quite active on the SLDev list (mostly in the periphery). Both Lindens and users can be seen as information seekers and suppliers contributing to rather specialist discussions. In the context of those technical discussions, Lindens also organize in-world open-source meetings and hold office hours (ranging from Q&A to round-robin format) which aim to extend these conversations and bounce off (new) ideas to develop and sooth particular objections that users may have. According to the Linden interviewees, however, users do not tend to have burning questions; instead they like to hang out and ask curious questions.

As explained earlier, JIRA is used as a tool to help organize tasks internally. There is also a public version that is used to collect and organize user input (which is connected to the internal JIRA). Lindens regularly interact with users by posting comments and posing questions regarding all kinds of issues. More specifically, it is the main method that Lindens

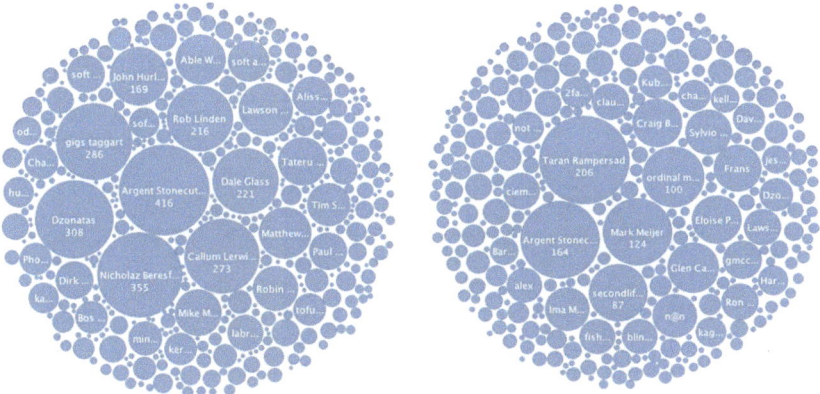

Fig. 5.4 Mailing lists: SLDev and secondlifescripters

use to quickly root out issues entered by users such as bugs and feature requests, and to determine how these should be actioned, such as which Lindens should be informed, whether users should be notified and an estimated timeframe for a resolution. Yet, some critical voices complain about JIRA's user friendliness and the slow pace of assigning and/or resolving issues:

> The thing is, people think we don't listen, but some stuff just takes time. [...] But there's really no percentage in us saying we're working on it. We have tons of people actually working on it. [...] It's an insanely complicated problem, and we have to make sure we make it better, not worse. [...] The frustrating part is that there's no useful way to express that to the residents. People want their problems fixed, and they want it now. I understand that. We all do. (Q)

The analysis of the public JIRA showed that 1516 users and 51 Lindens entered 3227 issues between January 2007 and February 2008. Most entries have remained unassigned (regardless of the number of votes an entry may have received) as can be concluded from looking at the numerous users who report to JIRA (left) and those reports that get assigned a Linden or mod developer[10] to be solved (right) in Fig. 5.5.

Weekly triage meetings further the prioritization of outstanding issues. These meetings are open to all users yet tend to be (virtually) attended by about 15–20 more advanced mod developers and usually not more than a handful Lindens. The agenda can be set by Lindens and/or users to discuss (recent) issues that get prioritized during these collective meetings

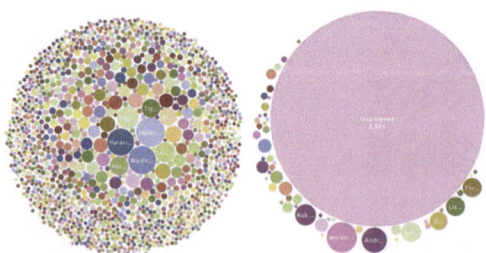

Fig. 5.5   JIRA reporters and assignees

for integration in Linden Lab's internal JIRA. Criteria include the overall impact on general usage, number of JIRA votes and the quality of (user-) provided documented information. The motivation for users to participate in triage meetings was aptly summarized by Warkirby, 'to learn, to shape the future of SL, and to make things better in general'.

Not all firm-user learning opportunities happen online. Linden Lab also runs the SLViews programme, which invites users to the San Francisco office where they spend a few days discussing specific topics such as griefing prevention, new scripting features, Windlight and several policy changes. There are usually 10–16 participants that may come from all over the world. Under a non-disclosure agreement participants tend to be presented with unannounced plans to which they can voice their opinions. For example, one group consisted of client-hackers and super-scripters who spent an afternoon with the firm's former CTO and open-source director discussing open sourcing. One participant recalls:

The one I was invited to was very techie heavy, the new physics engine, graphics, etc. [...] The SLViews thing was to some extent about figuring out priorities for what LL should work on. Currently they're just trying to get [Havok-4] up and running but there are ideas for what to do next once it is running. So its good to ask residents about what technology is being used for what things people would really like to be able to do and so on. These are issues that many Lindens don't really have first hand experience with because they're developing the platform rather than using it. (Seifert)

All these communicative means facilitate interactions between the developer firm and mod developers, highlighting various opportunities for learning. The next section describes several learning examples.

Illustrations of Learning Opportunities

Participation patterns and communication behaviour, to various degrees, organize people to share knowledge and expertise creating opportunities for learning to take place. Dan, a participant in OpenSim, describes what he has learned:

[..] I'll explain something about physics, they'll explain something about network protocols that I didn't know that I need to know. [...] I'm learning C Sharp, which I never wrote in before [...]. And I actually have learned things about the technology I wouldn't know if I hadn't worked on it, just how complicated some of these issues are, the networking issues, the physics issues. You know, I have a really good vision now for what's the scope of a project like this. Why it's difficult. Why [...] it doesn't get written in a couple months by a kid on the weekends, right? And that helps me think a little bit about sort of the business side of it.

Users come up with ideas, suggestions and solutions that are often need-related. An illustration is LSL workarounds, for example, working around quirks associated with functions used to interact with Second Life such as moving a prim from one location to another. A particular script (llSetPos) is needed, but it only allows movement within 10 meters, which is inconvenient for larger distances because the function needs to be repeatedly used. Therefore, some scripters came up with workarounds that were the result of trial and error and discussions with peers using, especially, the scripters mailing list and forums. In particular, interviewee Strife is well-known among scripters and Lindens for his developmental and writing contributions to the LSL portal. He won the 2007 Linden Lab innovation award for Best Community Organizer.

I think my opinions are received well. I have influence as long as I don't overuse it. My moderationship gives me some sway but I have the most swing in the LSL community. I've designed the spec for several LSL functions. I defined how all string and list functions should handle negative indexes (except for llInsertString). I wrote the test cases for llEscapeURL and llUnescapeURL (not that I'm happy with the implementation of those two functions).

In turn, Linden Lab may learn from such solution-based workarounds. Not only in terms of the actual solution, but such contributions also inform the firm about what frustrates users about scripting, what can be improved and possible means supporting this improvement.

Occasionally, micro, meso and macro mods may transgress the conditions set by the developer firm. A process of negotiating design norms may then be initiated. For example, the 'libsecondlife' project discovered an exploit[11] in Second Life where the object size was set to 10 meters on the client-side yet the server refrained from checking the size of the object with the client. As a result, big prims (or, 'megaprims') were generated that could be used for, among other things, construction, decoration and griefing purposes. Linden Lab fixed this but there were already many megaprims used (and copied) in-world. As these are quite hard to remove without breaking content, they can still be found in-world but are unsupported by Linden Lab (on a side note: several Lindens have used megaprims to build their office on the mainland!). Then with the implementation of a new physics engine megaprims started causing some problems. As a result, Linden Lab consulted with the user base—'to learn from the residents' (Andrew)—via SLViews, the blog and forums to discuss the future (or workarounds) of megaprims. In over 700 messages users offered their opinions about wanting to keep or get rid of megaprims and engaged in discussions, sharing solutions on how to effectively deal with existing nuisances.

Lindens have also shown an interest in open-source initiatives on the macro-level design space. One of the interviewees who contributes his scripting expertise to OpenSim was approached by Linden Lab to make sure their scripting was in tune.

> We spoke 3, 4 months ago or something briefly about the direction that I'm heading in with my script engine, and they had not released anything then. Now they released a few weeks ago a better test version of their new scripting engine, and he contacted me again so that we could get our scripts to be compatible. (Tedd)

Although the Second Life server is not formally open sourced, Linden Lab has developed a strong interest in such third party initiatives to discover what it can learn, especially in the case that open sourcing is not a guaranteed success. Moreover, the Linden interviewees regarded learning about what users are working on as a means to assist Linden Lab to strategize and prioritize work internally. In the case of open sourcing the Second Life Viewer, Linden Lab hoped to prevent mod developers from working on conflicting standards and, more importantly, to have them support platform development by outsourcing part of the work to users. In particular, open-source guides users to develop many (low-level) features, at least temporarily, allowing Linden Lab to mainly concentrate on scalability issues and the like.

There seems to be a strong awareness at Linden Lab that a lot can be learned from various Second Life users that use different channels. Many of the active mod developers are well-known to the firm and are credited for their contributions. Yet, the downside seems to be Linden Lab's lack of human resources to react and respond to the information it receives from user innovations:

> At the moment the SL client is open source and a bunch of non-linden-lab developers are playing with it, fixing bugs. Unfortunately, we haven't been able to throw enough internal resources at processing the incoming patches. There are a few Linden Lab developers who do try to import the suggested patches, but I think we're understaffed in that area. As a result, the SLDev members have trouble getting big projects done on the codebase. I think we could keep 2 or 3 developers busy full time just helping the SLDev people help us. (Andrew)

In this view, Linden Lab functions as a bottleneck, while Lindens can be said to be 'working in a fishbowl'. The functionalities of the design space and more general tools such as the former Feature Voting Tool that was replaced by JIRA and open-source initiatives suggest Linden Lab's intentions to be open and transparent, yet, simultaneously, seems to make clear the issue of Linden Lab's (in)ability to learn from its users in contrast to the user's ability to teach Linden Lab. As a result, by lacking the human resources to follow up on its good intentions, some bad feelings were engendered within the Second Life community. In other words, expectations between Linden Lab and the user base did not always seem to converge. Both the developer firm and mod developers needed to give and take so as to build a robust and functional platform, making Second Life a case that illustrates 'learning while doing' across firm boundaries.

> There have been a couple of cases when I've needed to know exactly what is going on in the background code. Now that the client is open source I

can check it out myself [...]. Generally though, if it's something pretty obscure, a given linden isn't likely to know that much more about it than the content creator residents. (Seifert)

I don't exactly feel like there are people in charge at Linden Lab. It's more like there's sort of a cacophony of ideas, and a general direction. [...] So you can often find someone at Linden Labs, I mean, I talked to somebody at Linden Labs about physics, and it was just like, you know, it was like talking to somebody at my own company. It's like, "Yeah, you know, this was hard. Yeah, it's pretty difficult." (Dan)

Linden Lab, therefore, may have promised more learning from the Second Life community than it could actually assimilate.

5.6   Conclusion: Complex Learning

This chapter has focused on user participation on the firm-hosted platform by highlighting aspects of learning (within and) across firm boundaries. In this view, Second Life not only functions as product and outcome of mod development but also as a site where the firm can be seen to learn. This is underpinned by interdependent dynamics of the organization of people, knowledge and resources across firm boundaries. The analysis has indicated that Linden Lab is not a firm that seeks to live in an ivory tower, which can be evidenced in the firm's strong awareness of its dependency on user base as consumers as well as mod developers.

Linden Lab has recognized the pivotal role of user input and has sought ways to harvest the full potential of user-based resources by putting various mechanisms in place that inform and organize knowledge contributions associated with mod development on the firm-hosted platform. First, the findings drew out several general aspects of knowledge contributions made by Second Life users. Several key factors were identified that assisted in approaching mod development as a learning dynamic, respectively, meta, scripting, in-world orientation, building and texturing, organizational character, features (and tools), other-directedness and perceived innovative character. The empirical analysis of information and communication patterns showed that the blog, forums and in-world messaging were the most frequently used means of information retrieval. The mailing lists scored moderately, while open-source-related knowledge contributions did not play a main role.

How do these results relate to the earlier findings concerning the design capabilities and design space? The findings can be connected with the six Second Life membership types. Power Rezzers and Functionalists indicated an interest in engaging in open-source practices. Their communication behaviour showed that Power Rezzers maintain a strong involvement in retrieving and supplying information to the various channels, while Functionalists expressed an active engagement in, mainly, information retrieval. Based on their mod development interaction patterns these two memberships are capable of developing iterated innovations on the meso level and, possibly, contextual innovation on the macro level of mod development. The Pro, Facilitator and Experience Broker memberships engage in performative innovation, while the Newb operates in the margins of the micro-level design space. And, whereas the Newb hardly connects to the community, the other clusters do engage in various communicative activities. The Pro is a frequent user of in-world messaging and, to a lesser extent, forums, while the Experience Broker has some interest in information retrieval of in-world group messages, the blog and forums. The Facilitator strongly invests in retrieving rather than supplying information on the blog, forums and in-world messages.

In the context of these findings, several documents were more closely examined with the aim of highlighting interactions between the developer firm and users underlying opportunities for learning relationships to form. The findings indicated that knowledge contributions tended to be made via the blog, forums, JIRA, mailing lists and SLViews. There is, therefore, no single representative communication venue and, more importantly, each seems to attract its own particular subset of the Second Life community. This seems to be consistent with the results presented in Chaps. 3 and 4, where different Second Life memberships were shown to operate on the micro, meso and macro levels of mod development. Some users may operate on more or all three levels, however, based on the findings presented in the previous chapters, it seems that users tend to work within a particular setting of the NCoP; each with their own levels of mastery and leadership. More importantly, meso and macro mod development appears to be connected to the SLDev and scripters mailing lists and JIRA, while micro mod development seems to be mainly associated with the forums.

As a consequence of the 'cutting up' of communication means and a high volume a weakening of learning opportunities can be detected. Moreover, the findings also confirm and extend the findings relating to design capabilities by indicating that mod development in Second Life is constituted by multiple centres of activity. Figure 5.6 presents the learning dynamic associated with user participation in Second Life.

This schematic of the architecture of user participation on the firm-hosted platform shows that most users operate on the micro-level design space, while the smallest group consists of the most advanced mod developers. In fact, users seem to master and work around their particular interest of mod development creating a centripetal effect. This seems to complicate the way sustainable relationships are formed and maintained between Linden Lab and mod developers on the Second Life platform

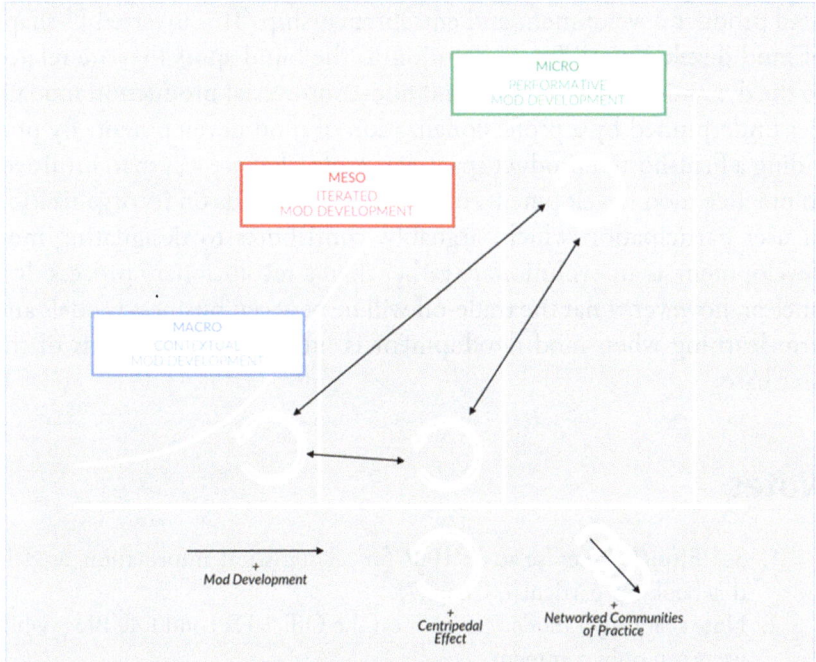

Fig. 5.6 Mod development on the firm-hosted platform

that underlie complex learning practices across (firm) boundaries. Furthermore, Linden Lab's system of distributed learning between mod developers and the developer firm has tended to generate many knowledge contributions that the firm seems incapable of effectively dealing with and, subsequently, risks becoming knowledge that is derivative. This refers particularly to Linden Lab that uses and reuses various information sources such as the internal and external JIRA and triage meetings for bug fixes, which may result in a decrease in the quality of information and effectiveness of user contributions. More specifically, the findings also suggested that there seems to be a point at which too many learning opportunities for Linden Lab may result in a 'bottleneck', which may result in stagnating development and user dissatisfaction and, arguably, increasingly motivate users to 'do it themselves' (see 'participation tipping point' in Sect. 3.7).

These problems do not necessarily stem from Linden Lab's practices. Rather they may be derived from users' preferences and practices that as a collective may work to damage Linden Lab's goals concerning distributed product development and entrepreneurship. This inverted U-shape of mod development draws attention to the blind spots that are related to the dynamics of commercial and non-commercial production modalities underpinned by a professionalization of mod development. By providing a firm-hosted product space and tools (that are less than intuitive) to practice mod development, firm learning depends on its organization of user participation which, arguably, contributes to designating mod development as an evolutionary rather than a revolutionary process. It is unclear, however, what the trade-off will be between business models and firm learning when mod development is fully put in the hands of the user base.

Notes

1. See http://etheses.lse.ac.uk/100/ for all statistical information used in this book (in particular, Chap. 7).
2. Note that only Lindens can post on the Official Second Life Blog, while users can only comment.

3. First, 65 items were checked for their suitability by screening for high correlations ($R < .9$) and significance values over .05 ($N = 421$). This led to the removal of one item ('pretend to be someone else'). The Kaiser-Meyer-Olkin value was .850 and Bartlett's Test of Sphericity was highly significant ($p < .001$), both indicating a good sampling adequacy. The PCA revealed 15 components with eigenvalues exceeding 1. The first component explained 17.4% of the total variance and all components combined, explained 64.3% of the total variance. A closer inspection of the scree plot and running the Monte Carlo parallel analysis indicated that the first eight eigenvalues for the randomly generated data matrix scored below the observed eigenvalues from the reduced matrix of the Second Life data. As a result, it was decided to retain eight components. Together they accounted for 50.68% of the total variance. A Varimax rotation was used to help in interpreting the components. An Oblimin rotation was conducted as well so as to ensure there were no correlations between factors. This was confirmed by the pattern matrix.

4. Note: results describe the explained variance and the outcome of the reliability analysis based on the loadings ($>.3$) of the items on the factors.

5. The other factors can be said to mainly concentrate on underlying structures of design capabilities, design space and organizational culture that were discussed in Chaps. 3 and 4.

6. As Linden Lab moved rapidly from a small-scale to a mid-size company it had to adopt a more formal structure to keep track of the division of labour.

7. A Linden picks ten tasks and writes an explanation why those were relevant.

8. Linden Lab received a storm of criticism when it shut down part of the user forums and started blogging in August 2006. Users complained about the inability to initiate issues, the danger of missing out and searching for supplied information.

9. The *SLDev mailing list* reported 410 subscribers contributing around 6000 posts between January 2007 and February 2008. The *secondlife-scripters mailing list* counted 370 users that accounted for approximately 3000 posts between October 2005 and February 2008.

10. Although most assignees are Lindens, there were six mod developers that were assigned nine reports.

11. An *exploit* refers to an unintended software bug that users can use to their own advantage.

References

Berdou, E. (2011). *Organization in Open Source Communities: At the Crossroads of the Gift and Market Economies.* New York: Routledge.

de Valck, K. (2005). *Virtual Communities of Consumption: Networks of Consumer Knowledge and Companionship.* Unpublished Ph.D., Erasmus University Rotterdam, Rotterdam.

Field, A. (2005). *Discovering Statistics Using SPSS* (2nd ed.). London: Sage.

Frederiksen, L. (2006). *User Communication Driving Firm Innovation: A Communication Patterns Perspective on Personal Attributes and Communication Types in an Online User Community.* Retrieved July 16, 2007, from http://www2.druid.dk/conferences/viewpaper.php?id=540&cf=8

Morrison, P. D., Roberts, J., & Midgley, D. (2004). The Nature of Lead Users and Measurement of Leading Edge Status. *Research Policy, 33*(2), 351–362.

van der Graaf, S. (2012). Get Organized at Work! A Look Inside the Game Design Process of Valve and Linden Lab. *Bulletin of Science, Technology & Society, 32*(6), 480–488. ISSN 0270-4676.

6

Second Life Between Participation and Competition

6.1 State of Play

In the empirical exploration of the ways the firm has arranged its sharing of the product workspace with its user base in advancing platform development, the user participation literature can be revisited. To date, the literature, particularly in the media research field, has largely focused on the firm-hosted platform as a site of participatory culture, pointing to seemingly transcending boundaries between production and consumption practices. It comes short of fully explaining mechanisms and implications associated with certain norms and values for systemic participation on the Internet. The work conducted for this book was informed by insights of the communities of practice tradition and user-centred innovation literature, to address such shortcomings.

In the sections that follow, findings presented in previous chapters are related to the dialectics of community and market. It aims to contribute an understanding of how a particular configuration of overlapping production modalities between developer firm and users is redefined. Several concepts are developed to identify this type of firm-user relationship in the context of the 3D software industry. More specifically, a reflection is offered on opportunities for agency and co-option as well as tensions

© The Author(s) 2018
S. van der Graaf, *ComMODify*, Dynamics of Virtual Work,
DOI 10.1007/978-3-319-61500-4_6

involved in platform design across firm boundaries, highlighting a more collaborative set-up on the one hand, with a more competitive one on the other. The relationship between the organization of within-firm resources and external resources suggests the likelihood for multiple centres of development-related activity to occur, where the firm and mod developers rub shoulders in different formations, moving attention away from the fluidity of firm boundaries to that of platform boundaries. A perspective is developed that takes into account emergent aspects of the so-called platformization of the Internet, so as to get to grips with shifting or new norms and mechanisms for user participation as well as values of creativity (or, labour) associated with trajectories of community and commerce. It highlights issues of, among other aspects, multimodality, contingent generativity, modification effect market and crossover learning opportunities.

6.2   User Participation Revisited: Qualities

As outlined earlier, the qualities involved in different participatory modalities in the context of commerce deserve systematic attention (cf. Beer 2009; Burgess 2007; Fisher 2015; Jeppesen and Laursen 2009; van Dijck 2013; Von Hippel 1986, 2005). The aim in this book has been to offer a rounded, more nuanced and realistic understanding of user participation in the light of the different creative capacities of users and variations in their contributions to firm-hosted product and platform development. An important reason for investigating Second Life members, therefore, was to build upon these existing studies that have provided parts of the user participation puzzle, but have yet to offer a robust framework through which to empirically examine user participation and creativity in this particular context.

In order to understand the kind of users who join and participate in Second Life, the investigation focused on users and usage. It showed that user participation in digital development practices seems to be motivated by social interactions, creativity and the innovation potential rather than a monetary aspect. This supports existing studies, which have suggested that users tend to participate in basic to advanced mod development practices when individual use benefits exceed their perceived costs (Behr 2007; Harhoff and Lakhani 2016; von Hippel 2005). Based on the analysis of participation patterns, communication behaviour and several additional characteristics, six membership profiles were developed; Power Rezzer, Facilitator, Twink, Pro, Experience Broker and Newb. These membership profiles indicate gradations of user participation in mod development activities, highlighting differences in creative capacities and the contributions users make to product development guided by the firm-provided design platform. Rather than understanding this normatively, this outcome contributes a *multimodal perspective* on user participation, offering a richer and systematic understanding of the various elements that underpin participation qualities in the context of the firm than previous user participation studies, and, to a lesser extent, the user-centred innovation literature.[1]

Previous research has suggested that particular technical organizations, often associated with toolkits, can enable user participation in product development by motivating users to learn, produce and share minor to advanced contributions. This can be cheaper, quicker, more efficient and of a higher volume compared to less user-friendly conditions (Jeppesen 2005). Therefore, this work further considers user participation in terms of the particular design and use of the 3D platform in relation to its enabling and facilitating of the development, coordination and integration of product development across firm boundaries.

The analysis examined how the firm systematically seeks to outsource certain tasks to users by examining particular functionalities of the design space underpinned by toolkits so as to provide a range of capabilities for different users. On the micro-level of user participation, the built-in toolkit was found to allow users to generate builds, scripts and textures. This yielded the term *performative innovation*. Meso mod development entailed client-side (interface) modifications, which are referred to as *iterated innovation*. Several external development initiatives provided *contextual innovation* by modding the server-side of the design space or macro level. In terms of relative size of these three domains, micro mod development encompasses the majority of mod developers and the smallest group of mod developers contributes the contextual innovations. In addition, it appears that the relative size of each level of mod development is not necessarily in line with the size of the contributions, or their importance to the firm. So, for example, only a small group may be capable of, and interested in, contributing to open-sourcing Second Life, which may have, however, a large impact potentially influencing the entire community. This seems to confirm certain claims made in the context of user participation on the Internet (Banks 2013; Bruns 2008; Jenkins 2006; Li and Bernoff 2008; van Dijck and Nieborg 2009).

In this view, product or platform development across firm boundaries, bound by several production modalities underpinned by a synthesis of user participation and user creativity, has drawn attention to the development and organization of the firm-hosted 3D platform in terms of 'modularity' and 'generativity'. Both concepts are related to a sharing of the task of production, particularly between developer firm and its user base. The analysis demonstrated that the Second Life design space is purposefully modular and generative in its design, allowing users with different skills and interests to participate in different product development activities. Yet, the possibilities for user participation in product development are not infinite (cf. Langlois and Garzarelli 2006; Zittrain 2008). Certain drawbacks, or limitations, of user participation on the firm-hosted 3D platform were highlighted in terms of technical, artificial and legal norms that guide the ways mods may be produced, transferred, integrated, used and compensated on the platform and across product boundaries underpinned by a mixture of proprietary, free and open-source software.

By investigating the qualities of user participation in the commercial setting of the firm, a more coherent understanding of user participation encapsulating status, architecture, organization of creative capacities and contributions to product development by linking the design capabilities to the design space has been contributed rather than focusing on different aspects of participatory mechanisms (Jenkins 2006; von Hippel 2005; van Dijck 2013). Moreover, this book has yielded the term '*contingently generative*' to contribute to the understanding of user participation on the firm-hosted platform as *a constellation of open and closed systems* that affect development and organization of product development across firm boundaries.

6.3   User Participation Revisited: The Context of Commerce

Whereas research has focused on user participation on the Internet evidenced in grass-roots communities (in many cases, understood as alternative or countercultures operating in the margins of commerce; cf. Benkler 2006; Jenkins 1992, 2006) and brand communities (in many cases understood as not-for-profit-oriented social networks operating in commerce; Antorini 2007; Tapscott and Williams 2006), user participation has tended to be understood as an expression of a DIY culture that can provide mutual benefits for firms and users. In this regard, several concepts such as 'produsage' (Bruns 2008) and 'like economy' (Gerlitz and Helmond 2013) have tended to emphasize a merging of firm/business interests, technological platforms and users. In other words, taking into consideration that some streams of thought have conceptualized user participation in terms of creative (or, cultural) emancipation while others have examined user participation in a business setting by focusing on profitability, user participation itself has tended to be associated with the notion of 'free' linked to social modalities such as collaboration and sharing. In many cases, users have invested skills, knowledge and time in digital development practices associated with a 'participatory turn' (see Chap. 1) such as self-produced short films, game cheat tutorials, page templates and fan fiction, without a particularly strong financial impetus. Against the backdrop of ever cheaper, faster and more user-friendly digital technologies, this kind of web-based user creativity has become more prevalent and businesses seem to have caught on.

The Web 2.0 model draws attention to the relationship between user participation and capitalism (Bröckling 2016; Fisher 2010; Helmond 2015; John 2012; Jordan 2015). Users in the commercial setting of the firm increasingly seem to have the capability to produce digital content, aggregate services, act as intermediaries and offer innovative consumption channels all together, customized to individual need and/or liking, highlighting a particular industrial logic on the Internet. This research was designed to yield insight into the various positions and interests of several players involved in a Web 2.0 business model by dismantling the development and organization of firm-user interactions across the firm boundaries of a particular 3D-software platform. Within this context the findings draw attention to the underlying premise of Web 2.0 business and production models that seem to be at odds with some conceptions of 'homo economicus'.

In the dominant discourse of economic behaviour, firm and market dynamics are often explained in terms of transaction costs. This perspective suggests that under particular circumstances people use a market when the benefits minus transaction costs exceed those managed within the organizational environment. In other words, transaction costs are associated with predicting—to the extent that decisions can be quantified—when particular economic tasks will be executed by the firm or the market, that is, the issue of 'make or buy' (Gudeman 2001; Rifkin 2014; Williamson and Winter 1993). However, the organization of production in many Internet user-driven communities, such as open source and fan communities, does seem to rely more on sociability rather than on markets or managerial hierarchies and there is no direct or future monetary return.

In this regard, the literature review presented in Chap. 2 has drawn attention to seminal works developed by Henry Jenkins in particular. Jenkins (2006) has pointed to a reconfiguration associated with user participation underlying business operations in the media industries, which he conceptualizes using the notions of 'participatory culture' and 'convergence culture' to refer to an intermediate zone of top-down and grassroots activities, and the unpredictable influences of media power and consumer power. Also, Benkler (2006) has provided a conceptual framework that understands user participation in the light of the networked information economy and is said to generate a likelihood of enhancing information quality and diversity associated with freedom and autonomy. In his view, the networked information economy works to enhance the efficacy of non-market production suggesting an alternative model to organize 'commons-based peer production'. This term refers to a framework of collaboration where 'inputs and outputs are shared, freely or conditionally, in an institutional form that leaves them equally available for' everyone to use as they wish outside the proprietary commercial system (Benkler 2006: 62).

Thus, whereas Jenkins seems to acknowledge and hail user participation in the context of commerce, Benkler understands it outside a commercial framework—as an alternative to firm and market-based models—depicting user creativity as a mode of (peer) production that is based on a kind of individual action characterized by self-selection and decentralization, facilitating social sharing and exchange, which are argued to underlie the networked information economy. This means disassembling positional hierarchies by finding alternative mechanisms to effectively coordinate people, back up from the privatization trajectory, and with a fierce commitment to ethics.[2] In such streams of thought user participation has been understood in terms of productive behaviour that, to various degrees, is connected to social modalities such as collaboration and sharing, which have tended to be associated with the notion of free resources or services in distributed and modular platforms, at least as far as users (or, consumers) are concerned. Thus, while such multisided platform outlook is marked by a more collaborative set up, at the same time it is said to also be a more competitive one, and currently indicating a destabilization of the dominance and rhetoric of user-generated content and user (social) connections, warranting a more critical outlook (van der Graaf and Fisher 2017; cf. van Dijck 2013).

How do these perspectives on user participation relate to the phenomenon of mod development on the firm-hosted platform investigated here? The organization of production across firm boundaries was scrutinized by examining work arrangements as a means to untangle user participation associated with 'free' in the context of economic production with the developer firm. This has led to various studies focusing on the very act of contribution by approaching user participation in terms of labour and play. Within the domain of games/3D environments the term 'play' has commonly been regarded as separable from everyday life, as something safe, fun and special (or 'magical') (Kerr 2006). Yet, with the increasing focus on user participation as production in the firm-hosted setting, research has tended to dub user creativity associated with 'free', as unwaged or 'free labour' (cf. alternative mode of production involving social sharing and information exchange, Benkler 2006). This draws attention to implications of production forces that seem to move from 'factory to society' (Terranova 2000), stressing that firms depend on those voluntary user activities. This 'precarious playbour' of, in particular, mod development has often been perceived as a leisure activity. Such an amateur or hobbyist status has tended to situate user creativity practices outside the professional domain and commerce (cf. Banks 2013).

Yet, the findings presented here have shown that user participation on the firm-hosted platform seems to be grounded in normative principles and values of productive behaviour and sociality demonstrating a complex interdependent dynamic encompassing both commercial and non-commercial interests between the developer firm and the user base. *The firm-hosted 3D platform as a site of participatory culture can be viewed as (non-) transaction locales that blend social and economic elements of production associated with product development across firm boundaries.* More specifically, Linden Lab's internal organization was characterized as a distributed design and distributed decision-making culture, which was associated with a rather high degree of openness, transparency and entrepreneurship (cf. Bröckling 2016). Achieving employment at Linden Lab therefore gave rise to a particular combination of requirements that, to a certain extent, can often be seen in the user-developer community. An important reason for this was that Second Life, encompassing multiple features such as the workspace and toolkit, served both developer firm and mod community, suggesting that a certain amount of know-how, know-what and passion were present.

In this view, the findings have demonstrated that user participation on the firm-hosted platform can be characterized by *digital entrepreneurship*. Not only in terms of development and organization of product development across firm boundaries pointing to emerging norms associated with an increased professionalization of user participation, but also in terms of developers who may be interested in monetizing their contributions (a 'participation tipping point'). These aspects point to multiple centres of activity, compensation and competition occurring on the firm-hosted platform. Therefore, I suggest that understanding user participation in mod development practices in terms of labour and play does not do justice to the complexity of the reciprocal dynamics among contributing developers, thereby highlighting emerging norms of participation and values of user creativity.

Rather, by relating the developed constructs of design capabilities to the design space and to learning, I have shown that user participation is evoked in a context of a networked organization of players, technologies and knowledge instantiated by particular modes of (overlapping) cultural, social, technological and economic production. As a result, not only corporate structures, but a multiplicity of non-transaction locales has been shown to underlie the business operations of the developer firm. These organize, motivate and inform product development across firm boundaries. This may render an industrial outlook on a reconfigured logic between developer firm and users somewhat limiting. Based on the findings, user participation in mod development practices on the firm-hosted 3D platform can be appraised as a 'connective market' (cf. 'social network market,' Potts et al. 2008; 'culture of connectivity,' Dijck 2013). This concept combines non-market dynamics associated with social networks, or sociality more generally, with commerce (or, market). Notwithstanding that aspects of sociability, innovation and creativity were found to be important drivers for users to join Second Life, the findings consistently point to the Second Life product as being in the 'production business'. In other words, in largely depending on user participation in mod development practices, Second Life's business is concerned with software and resources as services across firm boundaries and, hence, associated with the 'growth of knowledge'. User participation on the firm-hosted platform can therefore be identified as a specific segment of the 3D software industry or, in other words, as a *modification effect market* emphasizing that any contributions made tend to have an impact to various degrees on other users of the Second Life product across firm boundaries.

6.4 User Participation Revisited: Benefits

In the investigation of user participation on the digital firm-hosted platform, literature has given relatively little attention to the role of the developer firm. This is the case particularly in terms of the moving away from content production to providing platforms/services for user participation. The key focus has been to show the role of participants in shaping and maintaining a firm-hosted platform underpinning product development efforts from which the developer firm expects to benefit. Following a knowledge-based view of the firm, users are conceived as external resources of knowledge and skills providing the firm with certain inputs from which it may benefit (Brown and Duguid 2000; Foray 2004; Jeppesen and Laursen 2009).

In this view, informational inputs can come from within and outside the developer firm. These knowledge contributions may provide the firm with inputs, which may advance and fine-tune opportunities for (mod) development and benefit the product, and, hence, draw attention to learning relationships developing across firm boundaries. Insights from communities of practice theory have complemented the main conceptual framework to investigate such learning relationships via apprenticeship mechanisms in communities. Lave and Wenger's (1991) seminal work on learning models describes a process of 'legitimate peripheral participation', indicating an insider–outsider or master–apprentice learning dynamic. In other words, this learning model developed an understanding of enculturating newcomers to a community, whereby the relationship between long-standing members and new members yields insight into processes through which newcomers can learn from older members. In this view, an apprentice tends to participate in some kind of peripheral practice from which, upon increased mastership, s/he can move on to become an established and fully participating member.

In order to yield insight into learning relationships occurring between developer firm and users, this study examined user participation in relation to learning opportunities developing between firm and users, which underlie product development (Allen 1977; Frederiksen 2006; Nonaka 1991). Here, learning is investigated in the context of apprenticeship mechanisms, where learning, rather than being purely transfer-based, is understood as a social process shaped and maintained within networked communities of practice. Users as external resources can be seen to form an essential part of a 'constellation of networked communities of practices' surrounding mod development on the Second Life platform, highlighting different dynamics and interdependencies occurring among contributing developers (cf. Brown and Duguid 2001; Wenger 1998).

By linking knowledge contribution practices to design capabilities and the design space, interesting insights were developed concerning the relationship between firm–user interactions and learning opportunities and learning modalities. The analysis considered learning in the light of within-firm and mod-developer enculturation practices. The findings highlighted the roles of mentorship, the studio system and the mastery of various communication systems as important ways to embed newcomers in Linden Lab's internal labour process and also assist employees in career advancement opportunities.

The analysis of several firm-hosted communication tools and methods indicated that user participation in the commercial setting of the firm seems to underpin *multiple learning opportunities* between the developer firm and user base. Furthermore, empirical evidence of the various knowledge loci analysed—particularly blog, forums, mailing list and JIRA—points to differences in the appropriation of knowledge loci in micro, meso and macro development domains, indicating a *centripetal learning effect* rather than a linear effect as in the model developed in legitimate peripheral participation (LPP) learning theory (see the role of peripherality in F/OS communities in Berdou 2011). These findings suggest that *learning opportunities across firm boundaries can occur in all three domains of user participation* yet each potential learning dynamic between developer firm and user base seems to remain within one particular locus for participation. Subsequently, although the findings did not produce a sufficiently robust insight into the aspects of mod development as a learning dynamic underlying product development, they do suggest that opportunities for crossover learning across micro, meso and macro mod development domains, or 'cross-pollination' relationships, seem to be bound by certain thresholds such as the skill set that may impact on how firm–user learning relationships in general and user–user learning relationships in particular will occur.

Based on these discussions, principal implications for understanding systemic user participation on the firm-hosted platform as a significant aspect of the knowledge-based economy can be summarized by following indicative themes, which are ranked according to their robustness.

Differences in user experience levels are strongly connected to the user's (shared) participation in the development of the firm-hosted platform, that is, user participation can be characterized by multimodality.

By combining user participation patterns, communication behaviour and general user characteristics, a systematic and empirically grounded investigation has been provided of the ways in which users may participate, the types of contributions they may make, as well as kinds and frequency of interactions occurring on the firm-hosted platform.

By including a broader range of membership profiles in my analysis, the empirical findings demonstrate a more nuanced and complete understanding of typologies of virtual community memberships by connecting different users to a diverse range of experience levels, fulfilling distinct roles in sets of relationships forming between the developer firm and users, involving the modification culture underlying product development on the firm-hosted platform.

Micro, meso, and macro level mod development is a constellation of centralized and distributed, commercial and non-commercial practices, that is, user participation can be characterized as contingently generative.

The organization of product development across firm boundaries in terms of the functionalities of the firm-hosted design space highlights a delicate balance of user participation on the firm-hosted platform. A kind of a 'user participation loophole' seems to exist that points to a constellation of various degrees of open and closed systems that make up and underlie operations of the firm-hosted platform that may impact on norms and values of mod development practices in general, and entrepreneurial endeavours in particular (such as in terms of transferability and compensation). Consequently, claims of previous studies, which seem to give web-based user participation the benefit of the doubt in terms of openness, empowerment and subversiveness, can be conditioned. Rather, as was systematically shown, a commercial approach to user participation in firm-hosted development practices is open, yet it also has a closed meaning. By this I mean that the firm incites user participation but, by controlling parts of the design, implicitly encapsulates mod development as proprietary extensions of the firm-hosted product that may be particularly beneficial for the firm. As a result, a simultaneously centralized and dispersed, commercial and non-commercial constellation of product development practices exists that is (entirely) attributable to user participation on the firm-hosted platform.

Contributing developers have this constellation space at their disposal to work in, negotiate with and reconfigure as an essential part of the developer firm's business model.

Mod development on the firm-hosted platform is a multiplicity of entrepreneurship, that is, user participation can be characterized as modification effect market.
User participation on the firm-hosted platform can be characterized by mutual dependency between the developer firm and users. This makes explicit the arguments developed in the user participation literature that user-generated contributions create a particular logic between firm and user base, pointing to an increasing importance of interdependent production practices. In particular, intersecting labour processes across firm and (multisided) platform boundaries show a consistent relationship between the organization of within-firm resources and external resources, suggesting the likelihood for multiple centres of mod-development-related activity, competition and compensation to occur associated with entrepreneurship, where developer firm and mod developers, throughout the course of community life, rub shoulders in different formations.

From the perspective of the developer firm, relatively low investments are made in the development of the platform as nearly all content is user-generated rather than produced in-house, highlighting the firm's overarching business model that can be characterized by a particular kind of outsourcing (or, outsourcing 2.0) (see capital-intensive game engine development in Dovey and Kennedy 2006).[3] Furthermore, permeable boundaries between the developer firm and mod developers (jointly) operating in practice-oriented networks draw attention to the reduction of (production) costs, non-linear expansion and competitive advantage, indicating a strong entrepreneurial approach towards the organization of labour processes that may not only benefit the firm but also contributing users. Those users that are steeped in mod development practices draw attention to an entrepreneurial norms and values approach to mod development, highlighting opportunities for competition and compensation with the developer firm, in particular, and the community at large. This is what I have termed a participation tipping point where the developer firm increasingly becomes a client of mod developments, or a 'reversed participant'.

In this view, user participation is demonstrated as a rather well-developed business model in a commercial setting of the 3D-software industry. User participation occurs in multiple formations constituted by commercial and non-commercial developers. These are role-based and temporary because of the perpetual state of development characterizing the 3D platform. As a result, a dynamic relationship between designed and emergent practices is continuously shaped, negotiated, confirmed and reconfirmed among commercial and non-commercial contributing developers.

Knowledge loci exist that support multiple learning relationships to occur between the developer firm and users, that is, user participation can be characterized by crossover learning opportunities.

The insights produced confirm the argument presented in previous studies that the developer firm can learn from its user base in terms of apprenticeship mechanisms and information and communication practices underpinned by knowledge and expertise sharing, and the development, negotiating and remaking of design norms influencing the three domains of product development.

The presence of several firm-provided communication venues points towards crossover learning opportunities between the developer firm and the user base that work as catalysts of product development and which, subsequently, may benefit the developer firm and the wider mod community. More specifically, each domain of product development seems to be associated with particular communication channels, while each knowledge locus seems to represent a particular subset, with minimal overlap, of contributing mod developers, which points to multiple learning opportunities across firm boundaries. Furthermore, knowledge loci seem to be differently appropriated into the three domains of user participation, highlighting a centripetal effect underlying learning dynamics across firm boundaries. Hence, rather than a more linear learning model associated with LPP, learning tends to remain within a particular mod development domain, suggesting a nuanced impact of cross-pollination learning opportunities across the micro-, meso- and macro-domain boundaries.

As a result, this outcome might point to differences in the firm–user learning and user–user learning dynamic as the firm taps into all domains of user participation while users are likely to stay put in one domain.[4]

This model of distributed learning, however, suggests that the relationship between firm learning and the type and number of knowledge contributions made underlying learning opportunities has an inverse-U shape. Initially crossover learning opportunities between the firm and users seem to help further product development yet too much input seems to hinder firm learning (and arguably, stagnate mod development) as the firm's capacity to effectively deal with learning opportunities seems to fall short (and, arguably, can be said to fail to learn). The firm promised more learning than it could actually provide that potentially harms a transparent, effective and trust-inducing interdependent relationship that underlies product and platform development across firm boundaries.

This section has outlined the principal theoretical implications with respect to the user participation literature by revisiting the main findings presented in this book. The research has aimed to offer an enhanced theoretical perspective on user participation in mod development practices on the firm-hosted platform underpinning product and platform development across firm boundaries. The main conceptual contributions are the notions of multimodality, contingent generation, market-modification effect and crossover learning opportunities, which have been developed to conceptualize further the uncovering of platform development between communities and commerce.

6.5   Conclusion: ComMODify!

This chapter has woven together the empirical findings and discussed their theoretical implications in the context of the user-participation literature that is associated specifically with traditions in media theory. The investigation of user participation in the commercial setting of the developer firm has emphasized those relations that underlie within-firm and external resources, identifying, making up and leveraging multilevelled aspects of what can be called a *firm-hosted modification culture*.

The findings have developed a richer and deeper understanding of user participation on the firm-hosted platform, highlighting variations among creative capacities and contributions made to product development, guided by a firm-provided design space whereby several functionalities provide a range of capabilities, allowing for different user inputs and outputs. In this view, *a multimodal* rather than a *unimodal* perspective has been contributed on user participation in mod development practices in the commercial setting of the developer firm. Furthermore, the analysis of the structure and organization of user participation in terms of labour processes across permeable firm boundaries indicated an *entrepreneurial approach to product development* underpinned by opportunities for competition and compensation to occur among all contributing developers. As user participation on the firm-hosted platform was examined in a context of a networked organization of different players, technologies and knowledge, the term *modification effect market* was introduced to identify this particular configuration between the developer firm and the user base in the 3D-software context.

The analysis has shown that product and platform development is underpinned by *centralized and dispersed, commercial and non-commercial-related practices,* specific to user participation on the firm-hosted platform. In this context, attention was drawn to the role of emerging norms and values associated with several technical, artificial and legal aspects that enable, facilitate and condition user participation and user creativity in relation to the extent of mod development opportunities associated with the Second Life product. The findings indicate that user participation in firm-hosted mod development practices is limited in terms of *production, transferability, integration, usage and compensation* within and across product boundaries. A delicate balance of user participation in the commercial setting of the firm becomes apparent that is contingently generative, highlighting *an open approach to commercial mod development underpinned by a closed meaning* that affects the development and organization of product development across firm boundaries.

My interest in detecting a learning dynamic between the developer firm and users highlighted the developer firm's model of *distributed learning,* not only within the firm, but also with regard to firm–user learning relationships. The findings showed that various knowledge loci exist from which the firm may benefit. In addition, each communication locus seemed to represent a particular subset with minimal overlap between mod developers supplying and retrieving information. This suggests that *multiple learning opportunities across firm boundaries* are likely to unfold associated with user participation in product development. Furthermore, the analysis of knowledge loci highlighted a *centripetal learning effect rather than a more linear model* suggesting that potential learning dynamics seem to remain within the confined locus for mod development, which is likely to influence learning dynamics across firm boundaries. However, the findings also pointed to an important drawback for the firm in the light of having access to multiple knowledge loci for establishing learning opportunities. When the firm is incapable of dealing effectively with potential learning moments then the firm risks a failure to learn. This may *possibly endanger a transparent, effective and trust-inducing interdependent relationship between the developer firm and users* that underlies user participation in firm-hosted mod development practices and it ultimately may even cause stagnation in product development.

The overarching contribution of this book rests in providing an understanding of a redefined configuration of the relationship between firms associated with economic production and users associated with free and/or social production involving product development, or a *consolidated life cycle*, depicted by user participation in product development practices on the firm-hosted Second Life platform.

Notes

1. In order to fully relate and interpret this study's findings in the context of the lead-user construct more research is desirable.
2. Closing remarks Yochai Benkler at Ouishare Fest, 20 May 2016.
3. However, costs such as those concerning customer support may rise as a result.
4. Further research is needed to account for the impact of the centripetal effect for the firm–user learning relationship and user–user learning dynamic.

References

Allen, T. J. (1977). *Managing the Flow of Technology.* Cambridge, MA: MIT Press.

Antorini, Y. M. (2007). *Brand Community Innovation: An Intrinsic Case Study of the Adult Fans of LEGO Community.* Unpublished Ph.D., Copenhagen Business School, Copenhagen.

Banks, J. (2013). *Co-creating Videogames.* New York: Bloomsbury.

Beer, D. (2009). Power Through the Algorithm? Participatory Web Cultures and the Technological Unconscious. *New Media and Society, 11*(6), 985–1002.

Behr, K.-M. (2007). *The Development of Computer Game Modifications: Creators of Games Content Explored.* Paper presented at the 58th International Communication Association, San Francisco.

Benkler, Y. (2006). *The Wealth of Networks: How Social Production Transforms Markets and Freedom.* New Haven: Yale University Press.

Berdou, E. (2011). *Organization in Open Source Communities: At the Crossroads of the Gift and Market Economies.* New York: Routledge.

Bröckling, U. (2016). *The Entrepreneurial Self: Fabricating a New Type of Subject.* London: Sage.

Brown, J. S., & Duguid, P. (2000). *The Social Life of Information.* Boston: Harvard Business School Press.

Brown, J. S., & Duguid, P. (2001). Knowledge and Organization: A Social-Practice Perspective. *Organization Science, 12*(2), 198–213.

Bruns, A. (2008). *Blogs, Wikipedia, Second Life, and Beyond: From Production to Produsage.* New York: Peter Lang.

Burgess, J. (2007). *Vernacular Creativity and New Media.* Unpublished Ph.D., Queensland University of Technology, Queensland.

Dovey, J., & Kennedy, H. W. (2006). *Game Cultures: Computer Games as New Media.* Maidenhead: Open University Press.

Fisher, E. (2010). *Media and New Capitalism in the Digital Age: The Spirit of Networks.* New York: Palgrave.

Fisher, E. (2015). Class Struggles in the Digital Frontier: Audience Labour Theory and Social Media Users. *Information, Communication & Society, 18*(9), 1108–1122.

Foray, D. (2004). *The Economics of Knowledge.* Cambridge, MA: MIT Press.

Frederiksen, L. (2006). *User Communication Driving Firm Innovation: A Communication Patterns Perspective on Personal Attributes and Communication Types in an Online User Community.* Retrieved July 16, 2007, from http://www2.druid.dk/conferences/viewpaper.php?id=540&cf=8

Gerlitz, C., & Helmond, A. (2013, February 4). The Like Economy: Social Buttons and the Data-Intensive Web. *New Media & Society*. Online First. doi:10.1177/1461444812472322

Gudeman, S. (2001). *The Anthropology of Economy*. Oxford: Blackwell.

Harhoff, D., & Lakhani, K. (Eds.). (2016). *Revolutionizing Innovation: Users, Communities, and Open Innovation*. Cambridge, MA: MIT Press.

Helmond, A. (2015, July–December). The Platformization of the Web: Making Web Data Platform Ready. *Social Media + Society*, 1–11. doi:10.1177/2056305115603080.

Jenkins, H. (1992). *Textual Poachers: Television Fans & Participatory Culture*. London: Routledge.

Jenkins, H. (2006). *Convergence Culture: Where Old and New Media Collide*. New York: New York University Press.

Jeppesen, L. B. (2005). User Toolkits for Innovation: Consumers Support Each Other. *Journal of Product Innovation Management, 22*, 347–362.

Jeppesen, L. B., & Laursen, K. (2009). The Role of Lead Users in Knowledge Sharing. *Research Policy, 38*(10), 1582–1589.

John, N. (2012). Sharing and Web 2.0: The Emergence of a Keyword. *New Media & Society, 15*(2), 167–182.

Jordan, T. (2015). *Information Politics: Liberation and Exploitation in the Digital Society*. London: Pluto Press.

Kerr, A. (2006). *The Business and Culture of Digital Games: Gamework/Gameplay*. London: Sage.

Langlois, R., & Garzarelli, G. (2006). *Of Hackers and Hairdressers: Modularity and the Organizational Economics of Open-Source Collaboration*. Paper presented at the Druid: Knowledge, Innovation and Competitiveness, Copenhagen.

Lave, J., & Wenger, E. (1991). *Situated Learning: Legitimate Peripheral Participation*. Cambridge: Cambridge University Press.

Li, C., & Bernoff, J. (2008). *Groundswell: Winning in a World Transformed by Social Technologies*. Boston: Harvard Business Press.

Nonaka, I. (1991, November–December). The Knowledge Creating Company. *Harvard Business Review, 69*, 96–104.

Potts, J., Cunningham, S., Hartley, J., & Ormerod, P. (2008). *Social Network Markets: A New Definition of the Creative Industries*. http://www.cultural-science.org/FeastPapers2008/JasonPotts1Bp.pdf

Rifkin, J. (2014). *The Zero Marginal Cost Society*. New York: Palgrave Macmillan.

Tapscott, D., & Williams, A. D. (2006). *Wikinomics: How Mass Collaboration Changes Everything*. New York: Penguin.

Terranova, T. (2000). Free Labor: Producing Culture for the Digital Economy. *Social Text, 18*(2), 33–57.

van der Graaf, S., & Fisher, E. (2017). The Imperative of Code: Labor, Regulation and Legitimacy. In P. Meil & V. Kirov (Eds.), *The Policy Implications of Virtual Work* (pp. 109–135). Cham: Palgrave Macmillan.

van Dijck, J. (2013). *The Culture of Connectivity. A Critical History of Social Media.* New York: Oxford University Press.

van Dijck, J., & Nieborg, D. B. (2009). Wikinomics and Its Discontents: A Critical Analysis of Web 2.0 Business Manifestoes. *New Media & Society, 11*(5), 855–874.

von Hippel, E. (1986). Lead Users: A Source of Novel Product Concepts. *Management Science, 32*(7), 791–805.

von Hippel, E. (2005). *Democratizing Innovation.* Cambridge, MA: MIT Press.

Wenger, E. (1998). *Communities of Practice: Learning, Meaning, and Identity.* Cambridge: Cambridge University Press.

Williamson, O. E., & Winter, S. G. (1993). *The Nature of the Firm: Origins, Evolution, and Development.* Oxford: Oxford University Press.

Zittrain, J. (2008). *The Future of the Internet and How to Stop It.* New Haven: Yale University Press.

7

Commodify! And Beyond

7.1   Grounds for Play

Throughout my life I have sought to construct, deconstruct and recon-
struct my understanding of the world. As a child I was eager for the world
to be LEGO so I could take it apart, understand it and put it back
together. During my adolescent years, I built, destroyed and rebuilt my
world view by travelling while trying to find my place in it. In my adult
life, I have connected, disconnected and reconnected with people from
all corners of the globe, making the world more visible for me. When
Second Life appeared on my horizon, I came to see it as a platform where
worlds were being born. Yet, rather than experiencing a 'Eureka!' moment,
I thought it was quite funny—à la Isaac Asimov—especially when I discovered that I had to learn, unlearn and relearn tools and skills to create,
destruct and recreate the platform. Now a decade has passed since my
avatar Rocketgrrrl Tripp set foot in Second Life. With bad hair and prefab clothes she offered me a whole new way to travel the 3D space. I
encountered many friendly human-, beast- and undetermined-shaped
avatars and I was inspired, amused and bewildered by many divergent
conversations. I was struck by the sociality of this web-like environment,
combining 3D graphics and the laws of physics to inform seemingly

© The Author(s) 2018   **163**
S. van der Graaf, *ComMODify*, Dynamics of Virtual Work,
DOI 10.1007/978-3-319-61500-4_7

endless possibilities for user participation. Mostly I was in awe of numerous users engaging in all sorts of creation covering miles and miles of digital lands, a sensation that only grew stronger when I learned about users developing ideas, builds, business opportunities, services, new uses of the programming language and so forth, perpetually making, breaking and remaking the platform.

Being originally a film scholar, my interests have long been grounded in developing histories of 'old' media when they were new. At the micro level, I wanted to understand how technologies and cultural behaviours interact, how they are deployed for purposes of formations of publics (or audiences), representation and power. In particular, how audiences, especially fans, produce and sustain a meaningful understanding of themselves and their place in a digital environment that is packed with meanings not of their own making, underpinned by historical precedent to anticipate the 'behaviours of the new'. Where I used to observe and interview people at their home or at small-scale fan conventions (such as a rented beach cottage on the US east coast, sitting in a circle with their self-made videos, drawings and the like), I now also study people moving between offline and online spaces, as they follow or live-stream their interests or share their creations online.

In today's 'connected' landscape, modes of so-called 'audiencing' have thus become more diverse, seemingly providing a wider narrative of audiences (Livingstone 2012). Guided by a kind of 'digital prefixing', this analytic domain can be seen to intersect with an ever-widening array of social, economic and political activities as well as private and public spheres. Whichever way conceptualized, the media landscape is changing at a time where 'everything is mediated' and inextricably linked to fundamental changes in society, modernity if you will, facilitating opportunities for connections and participations to occur in diverse domains (Cammaerts 2012; Krotz 2007; van Dijck 2013).

Altering logics of practices, technologies and private/public organizations, that facilitate interactions between people, warrant a renewed focus on revealing and understanding emerging or changing conditions for present-day participations; particularly as we still try to comprehend what this ever increasing conjoining of our life with the digital is or could be (cf. Deuze 2012). Let us then ponder in the remainder of this chapter about the intersection of participation and platforms. The next section sets off by revisiting 'what is happening' at the crossroads of commerce and community highlighting and contextualizing the key findings presented in the previous chapters. In the section that follows, attention is drawn to public value as an important opportunity for further research in facilitating and sustaining participation, or online sociality more broadly. Some concluding remarks end the journey of this book.

7.2 At the Crossroads of Commerce and Community

With the investigation of the micro-systems and behaviours of the Second Life platform as a site, intricate tensions associated with the normalization of participation in everyday life can be uncovered. As a forerunner of a firm-hosted platform that thrives on user-generated content (or, data) maintaining a microcosm for Internet and real-life culture, Second Life has come to be associated with a framework for participation tightly embedded in diverse spheres of life and particular conditions and modes of 'usership'. The previous chapters have focused on improving our understanding of the way interactions between the firm and users are developed and organized across permeable firm boundaries in the context of product and platform development. The goals of the platform and the creative capacities, or interests of users, have been examined by focusing on the kinds of input that users can give, the structure of inputs, external rule sets and community-based norms informing the loci where development and organization of platform–user interactions assert themselves. Such an inclusive logic of revealing complex connections occurring between among others the platform, participants, participations and economic structures, have drawn attention to particular constellations that could benefit understandings of, for example, power relations, entrepreneurship and human development (van der Graaf 2015), while offering a basis to assess several claims that have been attached to the idea of the 'participatory web'.

The tensions concerning participation are evoked in an organization of interconnected stakeholders, technologies and knowledges played out by various modes of especially (overlapping) social, technological and economic production. Such systemic participatory infrastructure modalities indicate learning relationships between the firm and user base that underlie the business operations of the firm in informing and organizing platform development. These processes, described in this book, provide a deeper understanding of the blending together of contemporary social, or community, dynamics and commerce. Understanding this enables us to unravel emergent aspects of trajectories of platformization (where the platform is the dominant infrastructural and economic model with centrifugal powers), thereby also exposing all actors involved to new options and challenges that in their turn may impact these trajectories as they materialize (cf. 'platform capitalism' in Srnicek 2017).

Such a particular participation framework à la Second Life suggests a complex intersection of designed and emergent development practices attracting contributors with different interests, skills and knowledge levels. The presence of and access to various tools, support systems and learning opportunities enables and assists different users in contributing to, or modding, the firm-hosted platform in various capacities. Yet the sky is virtually the limit as it is boxed in the limitations put forth by Second Life. Some of these are related to certain user preferences and practices that may be contrary to Linden Lab's overarching strategy, while others may point towards constraints of a more technical nature. Moreover, the platform is mostly a work-in-progress where goals, appearance and usage guide a change-inducing result for the (configuration of) business. Such a dynamic of 'give and take' among constellations of platform developers demonstrates a consolidated life cycle that is simultaneously structured and emergent, top-down and bottom-up, centralized and dispersed, commercial and non-commercial. In this view, the participation framework can best be characterized, in order of robustness, by the concepts of multimodality, contingent generativity, modification effect market and crossover learning opportunities. The 'business' of participation, thus, seems to be more evolutionary than revolutionary in the context of today's 'everything digital life', yet with the challenging task for the firm to coordinate, integrate and learn from its users in order to nurture an innovative, self-sustaining product and a thriving platform culture.

As a dedicated platform for user-created content, Second Life has served as a pivotal site and facilitator of change in framing what is considered as 'content', who as 'creator' and where social and economic value is produced and obtained (cf. Burgess and Woodford 2015). The Second Life premise, therefore, offered here as a basis to assess and contextualize certain blind spots, or implicit claims, that underpin the shift from a user to a market-based perspective of many contemporary digital organizations. And now that the time to marvel at 'the participatory turn' is perhaps over, attention is being directed to more critical accounts of 'what is going on'. For example, popular keywords or concepts are systematically examined vis-à-vis discursive practices such as empowerment, exploitation and transparency (John 2012; Kennedy 2016; Mansell 2016a; cf. Dusi 2016). Also, awareness has been raised about the ideological paradigm shift co-opting communitarian ideas by the business discourse (van Dijck and Nieborg 2009) as well as about approaching platforms as neutral intermediaries (Kohl 2012; Marsden 2017). Be it creating or sharing content or just a simple click, all activity and data are likely to be 'capitalized, privatized and appropriated' (Gillespie 2017; Schäfer and Es 2017). What is more, some early evidence is available suggesting that developers tend to give insufficient attention to human behaviours in the (evolutionary) technical innovation process of digital platforms, that is, to how power relationships operate within innovation processes from a social science stance. Hence, they seem to run the risk of overlooking normative alternatives for platforms that are ultimately embedded in, or serve, social, commercial, military or political motives (Mansell 2016b).

Catapulting participation unto a 'stage of platformized play' demands systematic and critical attention, disentangling co-optation strategies of the various players involved, as this practice has brought with it a whole new industry of participatory measures, affordances and organizations (see mobile apps as important market segment in Nieborg 2015). Labelling something participatory (or, co-creative, collaborative and the like) goes hand-in-hand with a particular technical, economic and social organization of a platform steering the logic of deployment and experience and the like. What is more, platforms—for participation—are increasingly being seen or treated as a transformative means, a holy grail even, for many domains in society; be it ordering a taxi, booking a flight and hotel, taking online classes, accessing the news and so on. In their role as enablers, or a marketplace, platforms facilitate individuals (as citizens, consumers, users etc.), organizations and governmental entities to produce and exchange knowledge and to offer a meeting place for supply and demand (van Dijck et al. 2016). As an intermediary, platforms offer multiple stakeholders to take up, often simultaneously, different roles such as buyer or seller of services (see 'platform revolution' in Parker et al. 2016).

Increasingly, as pointed out in this book, platforms are facilitators of participatory or co-creative practices in supply and development, which are also becoming highly personalized. Connections made among stakeholders vis-à-vis the platform (and ownership) are in many ways conditioned by algorithms which, in their turn, make use of data collected by platforms about their users. More specifically, algorithms are regarded as a key logic governing the flows of information on which people and organizations increasingly depend. A complex ecosystem has thus come about of technical, economic, social and political interactions and conditions; in general terms, a platform tends to be seen as a technical, economic and social-cultural infrastructure that facilitates and organizes online social and economic interactions between various stakeholders driven by data (van Dijck et al. 2016). Moreover, as has been pointed out, platforms tend not to be stand-alone but are heavily connected (and ever-expanding) with other platforms, for example, by means of allowing users to use their social network login to access another portal site, or generating tailored advertisements from one site to the next, or deploying recommender systems via your digital data footprint—impacting the ways 'sociality and commerce' are organized in society today.

In other words, the rise of the platform as the dominant infrastructural and economic model underpinning the conjunction of our 'life and digital', data production is increasingly decentralized while data collection is recentralized (cf. Helmond 2015; Srnicek 2017). It seems to highlight a shift away from the 'creative' user to the socially connected user, which is indicative of a more controlled and surveyed (eco)system of monolithic, proprietary platforms (van der Graaf and Fisher 2017). It is this mediation and manipulation of participation, or creative and social relationships and the gathering of people's preferences (across the Internet) on an unprecedented scale, that impacts on, among other things, the privacy of individuals online. Thus, while some scholars have pointed to increasing empowerment opportunities of participation, others take a more critical stance and urge, for example, re/examination of current privacy laws or the capabilities people need to possess to access and use digital media and platforms to act upon an intensively mediated world (van der Graaf 2015). This issue and many others underpin this realm of market and non-market relations, a logic that plays an increasingly constitutive role in society and economy. What is currently at stake may, arguably, not be the commodification of the 'participatory' (or 'social') per se but rather how the co-evolution of the social (community) and business (commerce) relations has been framed. This, in turn, draws attention to public value.

7.3   Matters of Public Value, Literacy and Responsibility

The participatory turn has not only captivated corporate organizations but also encourages public institutions to look at the implications for their (digital) operations, including public services development. More specifically, the role of public institutions and the government can be seen as being that of a user, developer and regulator of platforms. A growing number of government entities can be seen to have an interest in technologies that tap into the innovative potential of citizens and improve interactions between government and citizens as well as a means to improve the transparency and efficiency of public institutions more generally (van der Graaf and Veeckman 2014). In recent years, political commitments have been made towards open government, in particular, and open data via inter/national, regional, local or thematic portals that make government data available to all, citizens as well as private/public organizations such as the UK Government (UK, 2012) and Flemish Government (Belgium, 2011). This practice affords citizen participation in using, repurposing, co-creating (local) information and services and value; 'It is a philosophy allowing citizens to provide their Government the benefits of their knowledge and collective intelligence through participation.'[1]

Policy documents such as 'Big Society' (UK, 2010) and 'Confidence in Citizens' (Netherlands, 2013) leverage this facilitation and optimization of public administrations and citizen participations as a core innovative process. In doing so, public institutions such as a city administration are interested in gaining better insights into citizens' local interests and needs, and deliver better services via smart mobile applications. The initiatives aim to enhance people's everyday life experience and further community development as well as to improve the administration's transparency and communication towards its citizens.

Thus far, the desired results of such a 'participation platform policy' tend not to be clear-cut or easily distilled, and relatively little empirical and systematic research on the effectiveness (e.g., substantive, economic, administrative, political, democratic, ethical) of participations and participatory measures in this context are available. For example, while participation tends to be seen as a mechanism to enhance interactions and learn from, or hear citizens, at the same time, it is said to be 'sold' as a mechanism that seems to put accountability increasingly in the hands of those who participate assuming that people will rely less on government involvement (see mental healthcare in Dehue 2014). Perhaps it is not so much the mechanics of participation measures as such but rather the performative quality of both participation and the ensuing measures that define their social impact—participation is of a communicative character associated with a complex set of explicit, implicit, wittingly and unwittingly initiated participatory activities arranged by government authorities to benefit society, further the political agenda and so forth. The choice of what is marked as participation varies with place, time and political party (and, agenda); more specifically, what issues deserve collective attention is ultimately identified and determined by the (democratically elected) government.

Against this backdrop, without much, if any, doubt, platforms and associated participation frameworks have gained traction in public and private spheres and are considered to be benevolent for society. This merits raising the issue of public value. What seems to be at stake is whether citizens and governmental authorities have sufficient knowledge or insight into what they can do with platforms, or what platforms do to them. Also, platforms generally tend to position themselves as defenders of the greater, common good, such as Uber presenting itself as facilitator of a more efficient taxi service and Coursera as making good education available to everyone. We have learned, however, while platforms are likely to make our lives more transparent and efficient, they also can give way to a more opaque system (e.g., infrastructure, business model, privacy) facilitating connections between citizens, or between citizens and corporations and public institutions.

The issue of public value here is ipso facto not so much about learning what specific public values are strengthening or undermining platform participation but rather about the mechanisms platforms deploy to determine and promote public values and the way they may steer or define the content and execution of them. More specifically, while platforms for participation tend to be praised for their intermediary role in facilitating among others social or economic connections and transactions, they are not mere facilitators and are not neutral but rather tend to offer a window or response to the way society is organized. Explicitly, platform providers set the rules and terms of service conditioning, for example, the kinds of content that may be provided by users, and more implicitly, norms and values are also built into the system and come about via, for example, the design of the interface and algorithms. A distinction in this regard can be made between 'governance of platforms' and 'governance by platforms' (Gillespie 2017). The latter draws attention to the issue of responsibility of platforms, in particular, when one considers how mechanisms seem to shape the way public values are being defined and promote a user's interest. Typically, in their seemingly intermediary role, platforms can play both sides, intervening at will, with more or less responsibility (if and how they see fit), yet operating practically and legally juggling multiple internal and external objectives and demands, values and regulations.

In this regard, a call can be heard to reassess responsibilities of platforms. The importance of designing tailored laws for different platforms (e.g., a social network platform differs from a search engine platform) is highlighted as well as to define platforms better in cultural, ethical, technical terms and so forth (Gillespie 2017; Goodman and Flaxman 2016). In setting the rules, so to speak, platforms and society at large are likely to benefit from a clear-cut approach to intervention and accountability mechanisms, when they should be deployed and by whom. The government on the other hand, has a responsibility to democratically define what are considered to be the public values of society and to look after them, such as values of access to information, privacy, equality, freedom of expression, prevention of exploitation and discrimination. Yet, with the changes taking place in the digital platform realm, arguably, the ultimate responsibility of governmental authorities (established and protected by local or national rules and legislation) is being effected. This seems to call for a rethink of their responsibilities as well, suggesting that the government should keep busy with setting the prerequisites or preconditions, quality marks and increase transparency of how platforms operate more generally (Mansell 2016b; Overton 2017; van Dijck et al. 2016).

The issue of public value then provides us with the opportunity to contemplate the roles and responsibilities platforms can play materially and institutionally vis-à-vis the public values or duties (and regulatory restraints) that can be assigned to these private organizations. This goes beyond the mere setting up of appropriate laws for platforms and allows thought provoking debates that encompass and impact societal questions and common principles, such as in case of controversies (e.g., from terrorism, to real-time streaming of rape, to fake news). Right now, this is what our society is facing and the response thus far seems to concentrate on platform providers that may be asked, required to (or not) intervene and which seems to fall short due to our lack to fully understand the mechanisms involved of how platforms govern. This raises many questions for us to tackle now and in the near future that move beyond mere 'commodification' ones, including: How do we better balance public value with the wants of commerce? In whose interest? Who is responsible for the implementation and shape of public value in this context?

Seeking answers to questions like these, moves beyond revealing and explaining the position of 'platforms for participation' within an account of reconfiguring production–consumption relationships and social change. We thus need to reflect on whether such changes are or can be democratic, empowering, for users and the public more generally, or if they mainly boost the interest of established government or commercial power. This so-called participatory turn also has been said to facilitate and reframe our understandings of individualization, that is, the promotion of the self and literacy. In particular, a preoccupation with literacy can be detected, such as media literacy, digital literacy, computer literacy, platform literacy and data literacy (Livingstone 2010). This seems to suggest a (policy) discourse where participation equals literacy. Participation as a kind of policy of empowerment, as seen by researchers, may inform a policy of participation on the nation state level too, and, arguably, is associated with reframing the analysis of people's engagement with platforms in terms of literacy (cf. van Dijck and Nieborg 2009).

Looking at this more critically, this interest can also be translated as a means to decrease regulatory intervention by increasing people's knowledge and awareness in terms of basic ICT skills (rather than stimulating more critical and creative literacies). Following this line of thought, promoting 'platform literacy' may result in governance 'at a distance' thus merely a kind of indirect control, which characterizes neoliberal market economies. In other words, the interest in the participatory turn in contemporary society may be related to the neoliberal agenda that seems to require different, individualized approaches to governance, in order for markets to be liberalized, barriers removed and so forth. A skill burden on citizens such as parents and teachers, seems to be a likely outcome of such a strategy and one that is also likely to widen rather than close the gap in terms of equality and diversity.

Literacy in the context of 'participation and platforms' can then indeed be detected on various (political) agendas and in many disguises, such as financial literacy, political literacy (e.g., 'Brexit', 'Trump'), environmental literacy, information literacy (e.g., 'filter bubble') and health literacy (Dehue 2014; Livingstone 2010). More specifically, participation on platforms seems to parallel wider questions that seem to allude to participation as personal responsibility. Questions such as whether nations are solely responsible for healthcare costs of individuals who smoke or whether there is a lack of health literacy? Was the financial crisis of 2008 exclusively induced by a deregulatory regime of financial services or do consumers have some responsibility as well, that is, some financial literacy, when buying into mortgages or pension plans? In the context of such debates, we should think carefully about the consequences of our arguments, or even involvement. In particular, we should be cautious in our consideration of promoting participation and platform literacy and whether it equals a neoliberal push of deregulation at the same time, which is likely to result in unjust outcomes.

As shown and argued in this book, the answer is likely to be found in elaborating a cooperative responsibility perspective. Let's look back again on what Second Life has taught us. Its strategy tells a story of platform and service development cutting across firm boundaries where the qualities and roles of users-as-participants and the firm-as-platform/intermediary support the development and maintenance of this particular configuration between the platform and users. In this view, Second Life has been indicative of a definition of a kind of 'multistakeholderization' promoted by ICTs and based on a changed relationship between sociality and economic production (van der Graaf and Fisher 2017). More precisely, the Second Life platform operated by virtue of productive behaviour, sociality and other related principles. This demonstrates the complex interdependent dynamic between commercial and non-commercial interests but also a shared know-how, know-what and possibly even a shared passion. User creativity can be seen, to various degrees, to become professionalised or to lead to digital entrepreneurship. Together with other stakeholders such as advertisers, multiple centres of activity, compensation and competition can be seen to occur on the platform. Current regulation can clearly not do justice to the complexity of such reciprocal dynamics among contributing stakeholders as well as the larger, significant (social, economic, legal) impact on many sectors in society. Notwithstanding the question of 'value for the public' and 'value of the public' that is increasingly becoming apparent. Now is a promising time to address the present challenges of a fast-changing environment of 'sociality and commerce' and succeed in changing them for the better. With Second Life as a noteworthy forerunner, it highlighted the complex dynamic associated with user-based to market-based trajectories and what this may entail for users as stakeholders in particular. At present, what seems to be at stake is the lack of a holistic approach in a multi-actor and multisector setting, yet, this could help to achieve the much needed equilibrium between (economic) efficiency of regulatory instruments and protection from regulatory loopholes, and from the commodification and monetization of data generated through virtual labour.

Notes

1. http://openbelgium.be/2014/02/the-true-concept-of-open-government/ (accessed 11 March 2017).

References

Burgess, J., & Woodford, D. (2015). Content Creation and Curation. In R. Mansell & P. H. Ang (Eds.), *The International Encyclopedia of Digital Communication and Society, Wiley Blackwell-ICA Encyclopedias of Communication* (pp. 88–94). Malden/Oxford: Wiley-Blackwell.

Cammaerts, B. (2012). Protest Logics and the Mediation Opportunity Structure. *European Journal of Communication, 27*(2), 117–134.

Dehue, T. (2014). *Betere Mensen: Over Gezondheid als Keuze en Koopwaar.* Amsterdam: Uitgeverij Augustus.

Deuze, M. (2012). *Media Life.* Cambridge, UK: Polity.

Dusi, D. (2016). The Perks and Downsides of Being a Digital Prosumer: Optimistic and Pessimistic Approaches to Digital Prosumption. *International Journal of Social Science and Humanity, 6*(5), 375–381.

Gillespie, T. (2017, forthcoming). Governance of and by Platforms. In J. Burgess, T. Poell, & A. Marwick (Eds.), *SAGE Handbook of Social Media.* London: Sage.

Goodman, G., & Flaxman, S. (2016). *EU Regulations on Algorithmic Decision-Making and a "Right to Explanation".* ICML Workshop on Human Interpretability in Machine Learning. See rXiv:1606.08813 [cs, stat]. http://arxiv.org/abs/1606.08813

Helmond, A. (2015). The Platformization of the Web: Making Web Data Platform Ready. *Social Media + Society, 1*(11). doi:10.1177/2056305115603080.

John, N. (2012). Sharing and Web 2.0: The Emergence of a Keyword. *New Media & Society, 15*(2), 167–182.

Kennedy, J. (2016). Conceptual Boundaries of Sharing, Information. *Communication & Society, 19*(4), 461–474. doi:10.1080/1369118X.2015.1046894.

Kohl, U. (2012). The Rise and Rise of Online Intermediaries in the Governance of the Internet and Beyond – Connectivity Intermediaries. *International Review of Law, Computers & Technology, 26*(2–3), 185–210.

Krotz, F. (2007). The Meta-Process of 'Mediatization' as a Conceptual Frame. *Global Media and Communication, 3*(3), 256–260.

Livingstone, S. (2010, February 18–20). *Youthful Participation: What Have We Learned, What Shall We Ask Next?* In First Annual Digital Media and Learning Conference: Diversifying Participation, University of California, San Diego, La Jolla. http://eprints.lse.ac.uk/27219/

Livingstone, S. (2012). Exciting Moments in Audience Research – Past, Present and Future. In H. Bilandzic, G. Patriarche, & P. Traudt (Eds.), *The Social Use of Media: Cultural and Social Scientific Perspectives on Audience Research, ECREA Book Series* (pp. 257–274). Brighton: Intellect Ltd.

Mansell, R. (2016a). Power, Hierarchy and the Internet: Why the Internet Empowers and Disempowers. *Global Studies Journal, 9*(2), 19–25.

Mansell, R. (2016b). Unpacking Black Boxes: Understanding Digital Platform Innovation. *Draft Information, Communication and Society.* Https://www.academia.edu/30175620/Unpacking_Black_Boxes_Understanding_Digital_Platform_Innovation

Marsden, C. T. (2017). *Network Neutrality: From Policy to Law to Regulation.* Manchester: Manchester University Press.

Nieborg, D. B. (2015, July–December). Crushing Candy: The Free-to-Play Game in Its Connective Commodity Form. *Social Media + Society,* 1–12.

Overton, D. (2017). *Next Generation Internet Initiative – Consultation.* Final Report. https://ec.europa.eu/futurium/en/system/files/ged/ec_ngi_final_report_1.pdf

Parker, G., Van Alstyne, M., & Choudary, S. (2016). *Platform Revolution: How Networked Markets Are Transforming the Econom- and How to Make Them Work for You.* New York: W. W. Norton & Company.

Schäfer, M. T., & van Es, K. (2017). *The Datafied Society: Studying Culture Through Data.* Amsterdam: Amsterdam University Press.

Srnicek, N. (2017). *Platform Capitalism.* Cambridge: Polity.

van der Graaf, S. (2015). Social Media. In R. Mansell & P. H. Ang (Eds.), *The International Encyclopedia of Digital Communication and Society, Wiley Blackwell-ICA Encyclopedias of Communication* (pp. 1014–1026). Malden/Oxford: Wiley-Blackwell.

van der Graaf, S., & Fisher, E. (2017). The Imperative of Code: Labor, Regulation and Legitimacy. In P. Meil & V. Kirov (Eds.), *The Policy Implications of Virtual Work* (pp. 109–135). Cham: Palgrave Macmillan.

van der Graaf, S., & Veeckman, C. (2014). Designing for Participatory Governance: Assessing Capabilities and Toolkits in Public Service Delivery.

Info: The Journal of Policy, Regulation and Strategy for Telecommunications, Information and Media, 16(6), 74–88.

van Dijck, J. (2013). *The Culture of Connectivity. A Critical History of Social Media.* New York: Oxford University Press.

van Dijck, J., & Nieborg, D. B. (2009). Wikinomics and Its Discontents: A Critical Analysis of Web 2.0 Business Manifestoes. *New Media & Society, 11*(5), 855–874.

van Dijck, J., Poell, T., & De Waal, M. (2016). *De Platformsamenleving: Strijd om Publieke Waarden in een Online Wereld.* Amsterdam: Amsterdam University Press.

Index

© The Author(s) 2018
S. van der Graaf, *ComMODify*, Dynamics of Virtual Work,
DOI 10.1007/978-3-319-61500-4